SISTERS *in* TWO WORLDS

A Visual Biography of Susanna Moodie *and* Catharine Parr Traill

SISTERS *in* TWO WORLDS

MICHAEL PETERMAN

Introduction by Charlotte Gray

Compiled and edited by Hugh Brewster

Doubleday Canada

Library and Archives Canada Cataloguing in Publication

Peterman, Michael A., 1942-
Sisters in two worlds : a visual biography of Susanna Moodie and
Catharine Parr Traill / Michael Peterman ; introduction by Charlotte Gray.
Includes bibliographical references.

ISBN 978-0-385-66288-8

1. Moodie, Susanna, 1803-1885. 2. Traill, Catharine Parr, 1802-1899.
3. Frontier and pioneer life — Ontario. 4. Women authors, Canadian
(English) — 19th century — Biography. 5. Women authors, Canadian
(English) — Ontario — Biography. I. Title.

FC3071.1.A1P47 2007   971.3'020922   C2007-901794-0

Front Jacket: A page from a plant scrapbook created by Catharine Parr Traill
Back Jacket: A watercolour of a bush farm by Philip Bainbrigge
Page 1: Period etchings of Reydon Hall and a pioneer's cabin
Pages 2-3: Lake Katchewanook, painted by J.H. Caddy in 1867
Page 5: The first page of a flower scrapbook by Catharine Parr Traill, dedicated to her grandson, Willie

Produced by Whitfield Editions
Published in Canada by
Doubleday Canada, a division of
Random House of Canada Limited

Visit Random House of Canada Limited's website: www.randomhouse.ca

10   9   8   7   6   5   4   3   2   1

Printed and bound in China

With grandmothers
Affectionate love.
To
Dear Willie Traill.

Lakefield Douro
1891

Ferns Flowers & Mosses
from the Douro Woods
& Stony Lake.

Vested by Mrs C P Traill.
during the Summer of 1890

(Opposite) *Making a Road Between Kingston and York,* by James Pattison Cockburn.

A Timeless Fascination

THE STORY OF TWO GENTEEL, WELL-EDUCATED English sisters who struggled to survive poverty and loneliness in the Canadian backwoods during the 1830s still resonates today. Susanna Moodie and Catharine Parr Traill are far removed from us in time and taste: their ringlets, long skirts and copperplate handwriting might as well come from another planet as another era. Yet these two women exert a timeless fascination.

We are filled with horror as we contemplate their unfamiliar experiences. Listening to icy winds whistling through the streets, or watching snow piling up against fences, we wonder: what was it *like*? What was it like to live in a filthy, drafty cabin in the dead of a Canadian winter? What was it like to exist without chainsaws, telephones, cars, electricity, trains, microwave ovens, airplanes, computers or the Internet? What was it like to realize you lacked the skills a settler needed in this vast and hostile land: you had never baked, made soap, sewn, milked a cow, planted a vegetable garden, killed a pig or tapped a maple tree? And to know that if you didn't learn these skills, which in the Old Country were way beneath your social status, you would likely starve? In their two finest books, Susanna's *Roughing It in the Bush* and Catharine's *The Backwoods of Canada*, we find our answers.

But the two women speak to us in more intimate ways, too. Their lives touch ours. Many of us have, like these sisters, dealt with the fears and frustrations of settling in a new and unfamiliar land. Many women today agonize over the conflict between professional aspirations and the needs of their families. And I've met many siblings who confide in each other more about the milestones of family life (from children's births to spouses' moods) than they tell their own partners.

Susanna Moodie and Catharine Parr Traill were not the only immigrants recording their impressions of their new home all those years ago. What sets them apart is the vividness of their voices. Susanna's writings, suffused with candour and *faux naïf* wit, have a Bridget Jones appeal: she laughs at herself and others. She gleefully recounts the story of "Old Wittals ... the largest eater I ever chanced to know," who was accused at a logging bee of having scoffed seven large cabbages. Wittals' son loyally rushes to his father's defence: "That's a lie.... Father was sick that day, and I tell you he only ate five." Susanna also shares with us her despair in prose and poetry: "Oh! Land of waters, how my spirit tires in the dark prison of the boundless woods." Twenty-first-century readers, steeped in confessional memoirs, relish the chance to hear this clever woman's interior monologue.

Then there's Catharine, determined to make the best of things and, when disaster strikes, quick to be "up and doing" rather than sitting and wailing. Catharine is so relentlessly cheerful that it takes the reader a while to realize that her circumstances were, in fact, far worse than Susanna's. Thomas Traill, Catharine's husband, sank into apathetic gloom over the years; Catharine herself suffered from rheumatism, gout, sciatica and neuralgia; the seven Traill children who survived infancy were often shoeless and hungry. But dear Catharine always makes the Best of Things: she remains British to the very core of her stiff upper lip, while falling deeply in love with the flora and fauna of her new home. Her apprehension that the spread of roads and towns was eliminating valuable plant species rings a very contemporary note. "Man has altered the face of the soil," she wrote with despair in 1852. "The mighty giants of the forest are gone, and the lowly shrub, the lovely flower, the ferns and mosses that flourished beneath their shade, have departed with them." David Suzuki might use more scientific terms today, but the concern is the same.

The contrast in character between these two resilient women is part of their appeal, as Michael Peterman points out in *Sisters in Two Worlds*: red-haired Susanna, "sharp-edged and opinionated, ever inclined to soar in her enthusiasms and passions"; sweet-tempered Catharine, "down to earth, practical and caring." When I wrote *Sisters in the Wilderness*, I was often asked which sister was my favourite. I would reply that I found them equally engaging, and then I would ask, "Which is yours?" The questioner always had a strong opinion, but it was rarely predictable. Catharine's maternal and uncritical warmth may have attracted more male supporters, while Susanna's competence and creativity (she is the better writer, in a literary sense) won her many female admirers. Most of all, however, I was struck by how the sisters made so many friends across the years. Their journey from that elegant Suffolk manor, through the backwoods of Canada, to the upper levels of our literary establishment is not just about courage and humour in the face of adversity. It is also about many of the obsessions that are with us still. The story reminds us, as Canadians, of where we have come from and how far we have travelled.

— *Charlotte Gray*

In dreams, lovely England!
my spirit still hails

Thy soft waving woodlands,
thy green, daisied vales.

When my heart shall grow cold to
the mother that bore me. . . .

Then the love I have cherish'd,
my country for thee,

In the breast of thy daughter
extinguish'd shall be.

— from "The Lament of a Canadian Emigrant"
by Susanna Moodie

CHAPTER ONE

Agnes

Catharine

Susanna

At Reydon Hall

AT THE DAWN OF THE NINETEENTH CENTURY, SIX sisters grew up together in the enchanted Suffolk countryside on England's southeast coast. Their family name was Strickland, and their mutual passion was storytelling, or "making up," as they called it. Sharing romantic stories from the history books they found in their father's library was a pastime that knitted the girls together, despite a gap of nearly ten years between the eldest, Eliza, born in 1794, and the youngest, Susanna, born in 1803. Together they felt the attraction of shaping their personal responses to the written word, first as parlour exercises during Suffolk winters and later for newspapers, magazines, the popular annuals of the day and finally, and better still, for books. Remarkably, five of the six would become published writers.

As the second-youngest, Catharine Parr, later remembered, the family was not unlike the Brontës of Haworth, Yorkshire, a close-knit sisterhood of young writers living in a remote part of rural England. Catharine and her younger sister Susanna would emigrate to Upper Canada in 1832 and document in several books the challenges they faced as pioneering wives. The second daughter, Agnes (born in 1796), would become the most celebrated Strickland in Great Britain for her numerous royal biographies, penned with the steady help of older sister Eliza. Four years separated Agnes from Jane Margaret, who would culminate her own literary career by writing a life of her famous sister in 1887. Only the third daughter, the comely Sarah (born in 1798 and nicknamed "the Baker" for her domestic

(Above) The three Strickland sisters who would later become the best-known were drawn in the 1820s by their cousin, Thomas Cheesman. (Opposite) A Victorian relief at Reydon Hall evokes the history-minded young girls who once spent many hours in this garden. (Previous page) Reydon Hall today.

Southwold

(Above) The town of Southwold in Suffolk (right) was dominated by the Tudor church of St. Edmund's with its 100-foot-high stone tower. The Strickland family would walk into town from Reydon to attend services there. The grandest houses in Southwold overlooked the grassy green of Gun Hill (below), named for its six cannons. According to local lore, these eighteen-pounders were presented to the town by the Duke of Cumberland on his victorious return from the battle of Culloden in 1746. (Opposite) Reydon Hall's Tudor chimeys.

skills), felt no attraction to the writing life.

The Strickland family estate in Suffolk was called Reydon Hall. Built in 1682, it included a large house, extensive grounds and a number of tenant farms. Thomas Strickland purchased it in 1808, when Susanna was five years old and Catharine but seven. Reydon Hall is located about a mile from Southwold, a picturesque coastal town and fishing port that looks out upon the vast, rolling waters of the North Sea. On its South Green overlooking the stony beach, six cannons point to the sea from Gun Hill. Nearby inland towns like Wrentham, Yoxford and Bungay were accessible by foot, donkey cart or, if one could afford it, coach. Norwich, the capital of the adjacent county of Norfolk, was thirty miles to the north, near the fenny flats where the Waveney River emptied into the North Sea.

By the 1810s the Stricklands were well settled into their Suffolk milieu, even though their position among the local gentry was circumscribed by their status as newcomers and Thomas's background "in trade." Thomas had been a successful docks manager and importer at the Greenland Docks, near Rotherhithe on the Thames in what is now east-central London. When he retired from that business in 1802, he moved his large family from Kent to Suffolk, where he rented Stowe House, a Georgian manor near Bungay.

By 1808, Thomas and his second wife, Elizabeth (who was fifteen years his junior), had six daughters and two sons.[1] For several years Thomas searched the Suffolk area for a rural estate that would allow him to devote more time to his children and to provide the entire family with a more health-

ful environment. In purchasing Reydon Hall, he completed that long-anticipated leap, one that he trusted would also help to confirm the social aspirations he held for his family.[2]

Even before the births of his two sons — Samuel in 1805 and Thomas in 1807 — Thomas Senior found that, in order to meet his growing domestic costs, he needed to stay actively involved in business ventures. To that end he bought a home in Norwich and entered into a partnership with a coach-maker, even as he sought to oversee the education of his daughters. Seldom was a governess employed either at Stowe House or Reydon Hall. Often, when Thomas and Elizabeth were busy in Norwich, the eldest daughters Eliza and Agnes were left to supervise the teaching and behaviour of their younger siblings. Training his six girls in basic knowledge and practical matters was a project dear to Thomas's heart. Unlike most men of his time, he wanted his daughters to be as well educated as possible, and thus in later life to be capable, independent and responsible. This forward-looking scheme provided both parents with genuine pleasure.

For Catharine, Stowe House was a child's paradise of freedom and adventure, memorable alike for the indoor

Catharine would later remember her family's early years at Stowe House (above) as "our Eden." The property had a fine view over the River Waveney (below) to the town of Bungay (opposite). Catharine recalled that "the banks of the stream were lined with sweet purple violets, primroses, and the little sun-bright celandines." Agnes would put her memories of the river into a poem (opposite).

schooling and outdoor play she enjoyed and for trips with her mother and sisters to the nearby town of Bungay, with its lively marketplace and ruined castle. A favourite within the family because of her sunny disposition, Catharine also treasured fishing excursions with her father along the meandering banks of the nearby Waveney River. He would read to her from his treasured copy of Izaak Walton's *The Compleat Angler* as he taught her basic fishing skills. The charms of Reydon Hall would be many, but the blissful routines of Stowe House remained alive for Catharine and Agnes throughout their lives.

Susanna was too young to remember Stowe House, but she would recall her time at Reydon Hall with similar fondness. "The old mansion house," as she called it, held many charms for her, from the legends of smugglers said to have hidden in the gloomy cellars to the treasures of her father's well-furnished library. To Catharine, Susanna was both an eccentric child and a genius of deep poetic sensibility, one who often needed a calming influence such as she alone could provide. Unlike Catharine, Susanna was impetuous and moody and passionate in her likes and dislikes. Catharine saw her as governed by "an inherent love of freedom of thought and action." Although Catharine claimed they never quarrelled, she did recall that once, at the age of twelve, she had "struck her a sharp blow" after one of Susanna's fits of obstinancy. This uncharacteristic act reduced Susanna to tears. After Susanna's death in 1885, Catharine observed that "such an outrage never again occurred" and that their friendship had remained unbroken from their childhood days in Suffolk through all their years in Canada.

To the River Waveney

Sweet stream of my childhood still fancy will fly
    To the green sunny vales with a pensive delight
There memory wanders and pours forth a sigh
    To the spot that no longer may gladden my sight.

Long years have past by and new scenes displayed
    But none to my bosom a pleasure e'er gave
Like that which I felt as a child when I strayed
    And plucked the wild flowers that hung over the wave.

— Agnes Strickland, 1819

Sadly, Thomas Strickland was able to enjoy the gentlemanly status of his ownership of Reydon Hall for less than a decade. Even then, the demands of his Norwich business interests took up more of his time than he had hoped. By all accounts he was a remarkable man and a fine example to his daughters of the value of learning and self-discipline. In a lightly disguised autobiographical narrative entitled "Trifles from the Burthen of a Life" (1847), Susanna remembered him fondly in her portrait of Rachel Wilde's father:

The father of Rachel was a man of great scientific and literary acquirements. He was a vigorous and independent thinker, and paid little regard to the received prejudices and opinions of the world. He acted from conscience, and the dictates of a powerful mind; was an excellent husband and father — a generous master, and a kind neighbor … he was a good and just man, and his family regarded him with a reverence only one degree less than that which they owed to their Creator.

Thomas Strickland

Composing this recollection in Belleville, Canada West, in her mid-forties, Susanna recalled that her father took her enthusiasms seriously and made her think out any challenging position she chose to adopt. He advocated responsibility in whatever his daughters did, be it gardening, raising pets, reading or writing.

Life at Reydon Hall changed irrevocably with Thomas's unexpected death in May 1818. Troubled by painful gout and dogged by concerns about his financial situation, he died at age sixty, leaving his family bereft at his loss and uncertain of their future prospects. With the end of the Napoleonic Wars in 1815, Britain had entered a depression that had significantly undermined Thomas's steady efforts to maintain and build his family's fortune. A business loan he had made to a friend further compromised his situation. Although his will placed a debt-free Reydon Hall in his wife's name, the Strickland women soon realized that they would have to make do with very limited resources and try to keep up appearances in as dignified a manner as possible. The two boys — Samuel was thirteen and Thomas eleven when their father died — were allowed to continue at Dr. Valpy's Grammar School in Norwich, but by 1825 both had departed for the colonies, Sam to a farm near Darlington in Upper Canada and Thomas to India in the British merchant fleet. The sisters at Reydon closed ranks and turned increasingly to writing as a possible source of income. It had been their father's fond hope that each of his daughters might become a writer. Had he lived another decade, he would not have been disappointed in the results of his teaching.

The family buried Thomas Strickland in the churchyard of St. Margaret's Parish Church (right), which is only a short walk from Reydon Hall. His gravestone (below) records that he "departed this life on May 18, 1818 in the 60th year of his age." It also records that his widow, Elizabeth Strickland, who lived until 1864, is buried there, along with a daughter, Ellen, who died in infancy.

The Life Genteel at Reydon Hall

The purchase of Reydon Hall in 1808 marked the fulfillment of Thomas Strickland's aspiration to the role of a country squire. With its Elizabethan chimneys and Queen Anne gables, the rambling house's picturesqueness and spacious grounds captivated his eight children. The girls made the attic rooms their special preserve, and it was there that they discovered a supply of foolscap and writing quills with which they penned their first stories. They were thrilled by tales of the ghost of "Old Martin," the brother of a previous owner who had hanged himself from one of the attic beams.

He was also reputed to be the author of a poem etched in a windowpane, and Catharine and her sisters followed suit. After Thomas's death in 1818, parts of the house were closed off, and one visitor described it as smelling of "rats and dampness and mould." Despite straitened circumstances, Reydon Hall would remain the Strickland family home for another forty-six years.

(Opposite) Catharine etched her name on this window at the age of thirteen. (Left) Her namesake was Queen Catherine Parr, the last of Henry VIII's six wives, with whom the Stricklands claimed kinship. (Right) A beamed attic room at Reydon Hall. (Below) Though no family portrait exists, Thomas Strickland would likely have wished to commemorate his family in a painting such as this one, commissioned by another successful Georgian merchant, John Middleton.

The Vapour of History

"History hung like a vapour over the Suffolk scene," recalled Una Pope-Hennessey in her biography of Agnes Strickland. "For imaginative historically-minded children Southwold was indeed a link with great events." The Battle of Sole Bay, a naval encounter with the Dutch fought off Southwold in 1672, was one such event. On its anniversary eve each May, the Strickland girls would watch for the ghost of the Earl of Sandwich, who, it was said, could be seen riding through Reydon. This great-grandfather of the man who gave his name to the famous snack was killed near the start of the battle. The English prevailed nonetheless, and a series of large tapestries was commissioned in honour of the victory. During a later visit to Hampton Court, Agnes and Eliza were delighted to recognize the tower of St. Edmund's Church on the Southwold coast in one of the tapestries.

The nave of St. Edmund's displays a model soldier who chimes the start of a service with his battle-axe. Nicknamed Southwold Jack, this figure is mentioned in Shakespeare and is the symbol for Adnams, the celebrated local ale.

St. Edmund's church (left) is thought to have been built between 1422 and 1461, and the half-life-sized figure of Southwold Jack (right), dressed as a knight of the Wars of the Roses, dates from that period.

Six tapestries were commissioned by Charles II to commemorate the Battle of Sole Bay (above), and three of them were hung at Hampton Court (below). This palace was built between 1515 and 1521 by Cardinal Thomas Wolsey (opposite, top), an Ipswich butcher's son who once herded cattle through Southwold and rose to become Henry VIII's chief advisor.

CHAPTER TWO

Bluestockings in Training

EVEN AS THE STRICKLAND SISTERS DREAMED OF success in the literary world of London, the term "bluestocking" was not a designation to which any of them would have aspired. Originally coined for the habit of dress of a penurious literary male, the expression had by the Regency era become a somewhat derogatory label for women with intellectual interests. Unlike many bluestockings, the Reydon Hall sisterhood shared a strict commitment to convention, but they were well aware that more women than ever before were making their way in the London magazine world of the 1820s, and they were eager to see how they might fare in that milieu.

After Thomas Strickland's passing, only the eldest, Eliza, chose to forsake Suffolk for London. The rest of the sisters remained at Reydon Hall with their mother, visiting friends in Southwold and nearby villages and making occasional trips to London to stay with relatives. While Eliza rented a room in the city and single-mindedly pursued a career

James Bird

in magazine editing, her sisters contented themselves with the domestic pleasures and duties of country life. With Agnes taking the lead, however, they began to send out their stories, poems or sketches to the editors of magazines and the popular annuals.

Literary friends in Suffolk were particularly valuable resources during these years. In the village of Yoxford, ten miles from Reydon Hall, James Bird, his kindly wife, Emma, and their many children welcomed visits to their home and pharmacy-bookstore. By the mid-1820s Bird had established himself as a leading local historian and poet, and not only did he provide generous encouragement to all the scribbling Stricklands from Agnes to Susanna, he also invited them to join in lively literary and religious discussions at his home, where they heard the latest Suffolk cultural news.

The Childs family of Bungay had been close friends of Thomas Strickland. John Childs, a printer, staunch Congregationalist and independent thinker,

(Opposite) A view of Bedford Square, where the Strickland sisters would often stay on London visits.

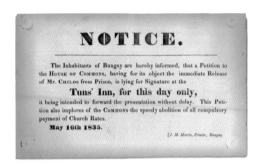

(Above) A notice from May 16, 1835, encourages the citizens of Bungay to sign a petition to the House of Commons requesting the release of John Childs from prison and "the speedy abolition of all compulsory payment of Church rates."
(Below) Phrenology was the passion of Robert Childs, John's younger brother. With skulls and charts, he would describe how character and intelligence could be determined by reading the shape of a person's head. (Opposite) Bedford Square has retained its elegant Georgian character.

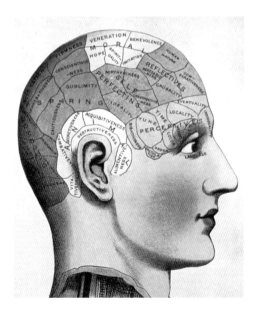

became famous as "the Bungay martyr" when he chose to go to prison in 1835 rather than pay a tax that supported only the Church of England. His drawing room was a place of lively discussion of subjects as diverse as religious freedom and current science. Robert Childs, John's younger brother, kept a "skull museum" where he entertained visitors and discoursed enthusiastically about phrenology. Catharine and Susanna were so affected by Robert's passion that, later in Canada, they each wrote comic sketches about his "scullery," which they dubbed "Golgotha." Sarah would surprise and disturb her sisters Agnes and Jane Margaret by marrying the eccentric Robert in 1835.

Another family closely connected to both James Bird and the Stricklands was that of Thomas Harral. He had edited two newspapers in Suffolk and was known as a writer of English history. His daughter, Anna Laura, was one of Susanna's closest friends and, like her, an aspiring poet. Around 1827, Harral moved his family to London to take up the editorship of a new literary and court magazine, *La Belle Assemblée*. The Harrals' London address was, for a time, one of the sisters' personal connections to the city, and *La Belle Assemblée* published many stories and poems by Agnes and Susanna until 1831, when Harral lost the editorship.

Two Strickland relatives, Rebecca Leverton and Thomas Cheesman, were also comfortably established in London and well known for their wide-ranging cultural interests. Rebecca, of 13 Bedford Square in Bloomsbury, was their father's second cousin. She was the well-to-do widow of the prominent architect, Thomas Leverton, who had built not only the elegant terraced houses of Bedford Square but also Charing

Cross Station. In the early 1820s Mrs. Leverton held weekly literary evenings that drew many of the cultural elite to her drawing room. She made a special pet of the precocious Agnes, inviting her to stay with her for extended periods. At one soiree, Agnes had the great pleasure of meeting Sir Walter Scott, a major literary figure of the time.

Agnes made her London friends carefully and kept a safe distance from the precarious literary world, with its sexual undercurrents and shifting reputations and relationships. Her flamboyant contemporary, Letitia Landon, a writer of romantic verse known by her initials L.E.L., took the initiative to become a friend, but Agnes was far more comfortable with conservative figures like the agreeable, middle-aged Jane Porter, a popular historical novelist of such books as *The Scottish Chiefs* (1810). Ever deliberate in gauging her own opportunities, Agnes soon became a contributor to several prominent magazines and many of the leading literary annuals that had come into vogue in the early 1820s. With an eye towards the importance of books to a young writer's reputation, she arranged to publish by subscription two volumes of poetry — *Worcester Field; or The Cavalier* (1826) and *The Seven Ages of Woman, and Other Poems* — for which Mrs. Leverton likely provided financial support.[1]

Thomas Cheesman was, in Susanna's words, a "perfect original" in his oddities of taste and habit. A bachelor cousin of the Stricklands, he lived and painted

Thomas Cheesman

in his dingy home in Newman Street.[2] In the summer months he often visited the Strickland family at Reydon Hall, and in turn he welcomed the individual sisters to join him and his niece when they wished to stay in London. To his fine representational skills we owe the only portraits of his cousins in their youth.

By the late 1820s, both Agnes and Eliza had made names for themselves in the London literary scene. Agnes was the more visible of the two, thanks to her outgoing nature and enjoyment of public attention. While she continued to reside at Reydon, her London trips were frequent and she actively nurtured new social and professional friendships, including William Jerdan, editor of *The Literary Gazette*, Thomas Pringle, a Scottish poet and anti-slavery activist, and Anna Jameson, author of a successful travel book who would later publish an account of her 1837 visit to Canada called *Winter Studies and Summer Rambles*.

The industrious Eliza made her reputation by hard editorial work. Initially, publisher Henry Colburn hired her as an editorial assistant for *The Court Journal*. She so impressed him that, by the mid-1820s, he appointed her to edit the magazine. As part of her duties, she wrote about the doings of the aristocracy and developed a series of articles on the deaths of English kings that can be seen as the beginning of the specialization in royal lives that she later shared with Agnes. By the early 1830s she had taken over the editorial reins of

The Lady's Magazine, where she used her leverage to make it something of a Strickland preserve for several years. Agnes, Jane Margaret, Susanna, Catharine and Eliza herself all contributed poems and stories with some frequency, and pieces by Susanna and Catharine continued to appear in its pages even after they emigrated to Canada in the summer of 1832.

As the youngest sisters, Catharine and Susanna came to their literary opportunities a few years later but by similar connections. Catharine was actually the first of the sisters to be published in book form. She was only seventeen years old when a family friend spotted one of her manuscripts for children on a table at Reydon Hall. Seeing its promise, he offered to show it to some publishing friends in London. A month later, he presented a delighted Catharine with an advance of five golden guineas. Thus, in 1819, her cautionary children's tale *Disobedience; or, Mind What Mama Says* was published by the small London firm of James Woodhouse, though it listed the author as "Miss E. Strickland, Norwich."[3]

Despite some long-standing confusion about Catharine's early books, the record of publications makes it clear that she had firmly established herself as a marketable children's author in London by 1820. In 1826 *The Young Emigrants; or Pictures of Canada, Calculated to Amuse and Instruct the Minds of Youth* was published. Stimulated by her reading about Canada, her brother Sam's emigration in 1825 and letters received from family friends who had emigrated,[4] Catharine offered in this small book a clear indication of her interest in undergoing such an experience herself. But soon she was on to other topics, several of

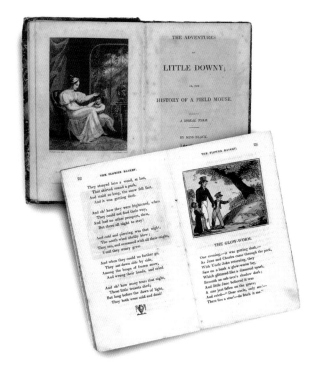

By her late teens, Catharine had become a successful children's author. Among her early successes were *Little Downy: History of a Field Mouse* (above), *The Flower Basket, or Poetical Blossoms* (centre) and *The Young Emigrants* (below).

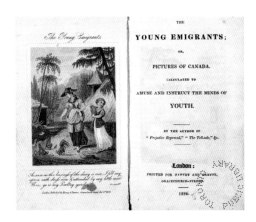

La Belle Assemblée,

OR

COURT AND FASHIONABLE MAGAZINE.

NEW SERIES, No. L., FOR FEBRUARY, 1829.

EMBELLISHMENTS

A Portrait of the Most Noble MARIANNE, MARCHIONESS WELLESLEY, engraved by DEAN, from an Original Miniature by ROBERTSON.
An elegant whole-length Portrait Figure, in an Opera Dress.
An elegant whole-length Portrait Figure, in an Evening Costume.
An elegant whole-length Portrait Figure, in a Carriage Dress.
An elegant whole-length Portrait Figure, in a Promenade Dress.

LITERARY CONTENTS.

OPERA DRESS.   PRIVATE CONCERT DRESS.

The February 1829 issue of *La Belle Assemblée* featured two poems by Susanna and a sonnet by Thomas Pringle. In the back of each issue were several colour pages displaying illustrations of the latest fashions.

which emphasized her interest in nature and natural history. In all, by 1831, Catharine had published twelve books for children, a remarkable number by most standards. At the same time she was able to place stories in several of the popular London annuals. From the very outset of her career she was a steady and productive writer, despite her limited trips to London.

While Catharine remained at Reydon with Jane Margaret and Sarah, Susanna was impelled to follow Agnes's more ambitious courtship of London opportunities. She, too, visited Mrs. Leverton, but her indulging in a romantic fling while staying at Bedford Square drew her aunt's strong disapproval. Like Catharine, Susanna made a name for herself in the early 1820s in the emerging market for children's books. Her breakthrough venture was a short historical novel about one of the rebel heroes of her childhood reading. *Spartacus: A Roman Story* was published in 1822, and she followed it with several other didactic works such as *Hugh Latimer; or, The School-Boy's Friendship* (1828). From the outset she saw herself as a writer of many talents, a poet and prose author eager to gain access to as many markets as possible. The correspondence she initiated in 1829 with Mary Russell Mitford, then famous for her entertaining *Our Village* sketches about her Berkshire home, was another of her attempts to connect with the larger world of professional authorship.

While the children's market provided her with a modest income, Susanna sent out her poems and sketches and eagerly hung on the encouragements and promises of editors. In 1830 she wrote occasionally for *The Athenaeum* (London) and curried favour with the editors of many of the popular annuals, bragging to James Bird in 1830 that she was to appear in a total of seven of them that winter. Like Agnes, she had learned that connections were often the key to publication and recognition. By 1831, her poetic output was such that she had enough material for a book, *Enthusiasm, and Other Poems,* published by the well-known London firm of Smith and Elder. Reviews were generally favourable, occasionally comparing her positively to Agnes, her even more prolific rival. By then, Agnes had become so well known in the literary world that, much to Susanna's dismay, several editors and writers confused her with her older sister. Highly sensitive about her reputation, she even experimented with a pseudonym, "ZZ," but, as this only obscured her identity even more, she soon dropped it.

In 1829 Susanna took a precipitous step that disturbed her family. Seeking a more personal religious engagement for herself than the complacent and ritualized Anglican church could provide, she joined the small Congregational church in Wrentham. Several of the poems in *Enthusiasm, and Other Poems* revealed her new religious seriousness or "enthusiasm." The young woman who a few months ago had been dutifully teaching an Anglican Sunday-school class, shocked her mother and sisters by her radical conversion. Indeed, this experiment — or "dalliance," as it was seen within the family — so offended Agnes that she cut off relations with her sister. It was not until a year later, when Susanna was in a grief-stricken state over the death of her friend Anna Harral, that a reconciliation was arranged. Watching the unfolding family drama with keen interest, Catharine was overjoyed at this "reunion

Jane Porter

Letitia Elizabeth Landon

John Martin

Sir Walter Scott

(Clockwise, from top) Agnes was thrilled to meet Jane Porter, as she had admired her historical novels since childhood. But she was more wary of the glamorous young poetess Letitia Landon. The most eminent writer she would greet in the Leverton parlour was Sir Walter Scott. The artist John Martin, best known for his large canvases of Biblical scenes, made a strong impression on Susanna.

of sisters" and hoped that, hereafter, "no worldly opinion, no prejudice, no contradiction of opinion on indifferent subjects [will] ever disturb [their] love."

Despite these differences between Agnes and Susanna, there were two matters upon which they wholeheartedly agreed: their passion for poetry and their unqualified patriotism. A tangible result of their reconciliation was a co-authored book entitled *Patriotic Songs*. It appeared in 1831 and contained four songs by each of them, set to music by J. Green of Soho, who also published the book. The "joint volume" won the "country girls" the praise of King William IV, who called them, as Susanna proudly recalled, "an ornament to their country." No doubt, she was quietly delighted to note that some reviewers praised her songs as much or more than those of Agnes.

Apart from Thomas Harral, Susanna's most important London literary friend and supporter was the poet Thomas Pringle. Through either Harral or Agnes, Susanna met Pringle and his wife, Margaret, likely in 1828. Over the next three years the childless couple became surrogate parents to her while she was in town. They introduced her to many of their literary friends, encouraged her writing projects and welcomed her to their homes in London and Hampstead for extensive stays.

In an 1831 letter to James Bird, Susanna excitedly described new aspects of her plunge into London literary society. For a few months while she rented a room near the Pringle's house in Finsbury, she found herself able to hobnob with writers at various events. She described her pleasure in being "her own mistress" at last and her delight in being treated as "a Lioness" at London parties. The soirees at the home of John Martin, the highly regarded painter and engraver, were heady experiences. "I am almost tired with compliments and sick of flattering encomiums on my genius," she reported to Bird. "How these men in London do talk. I learn daily to laugh at their fine love speeches."

Thomas Pringle

During this brief hiatus of independence in London, Susanna was never far from the kindly paternal advice and scrutiny of "Papa Pringle." As a young man, Pringle had emigrated from his native Scotland to South Africa, where he became a newspaper editor in Cape Town. He did not hesitate to speak out on the unfair laws and treatment imposed upon the indigenous people by white settlers, and his outspoken views led to his expulsion from the colony after a few years. On returning to London he joined the Anti-Slavery Society and was appointed its secretary in 1827. At the same time, he took up various editorial posts, using his influence whenever possible to help his young protégé Susanna place pieces of her writing.

Two life-changing events for Susanna occurred in the Pringle household. As part of his commitment to overcoming slavery in Britain and its colonies, Pringle invited several Caribbean slaves to stay at his

The Pringles' home was a London townhouse on Claremont Square in the newly-built neighbourhood of Finsbury.
For a time, Susanna lived around the corner in rented quarters.

London home while they acclimatized to a new life. One of these was Mary Prince, a former Antiguan slave, who lived with the Pringles in 1830–31. Under Pringle's direction, Susanna took down Mary's story, which appeared as a pamphlet in 1831 under the title *The History of Mary Prince.* Although not formally sanctioned by the Anti-Slavery Society, the booklet went through three printings that year and had a strong effect upon the educated classes of several cities. Its purpose was to alert British citizens to the injustices of slavery and to use whatever profits it generated to provide funds for Mary herself.

Knowing Mary Prince and learning the details of her story shook Susanna's complacency. As she wrote in the preface to a second pamphlet, *Negro Slavery Described by a Negro: Being the Narrative of Ashton Warner, a Native of St. Vincent's* (1831), her experiences with the two former slaves led her to recognize what she called the "great national crime" in which England was participating. Struck by the shocking details of slave ownership and moved by the simple and affecting narratives that she heard from both Mary and Ashton, she "resolved no longer to be an accomplice to its criminality, though it were only by keeping silence regarding it." In later books like *Roughing It in the Bush* she kept that promise, recounting several instances of thoughtless racism against blacks that she encountered in early Canada and making herself a spokesperson for more enlightened views.

The second life-changing event that took place at Thomas and Margaret Pringle's London home was the appearance of a dashing Scots soldier, John Wedderburn Dunbar Moodie.

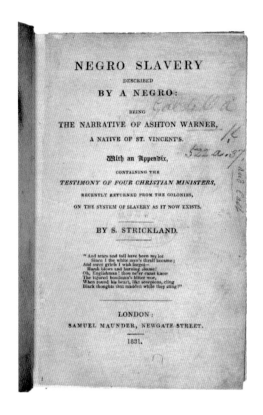

The Society for the Abolition of the Slave Trade was formed in 1787, and brass anti-slavery medallions (right) helped spread its message. In her pamphlet about the life of Ashton Warner (above), Susanna decried the "gross injustice ... of a free nation suffering such an abomination as negro slavery to exist in her dominions."

Sisters in the Metropolis

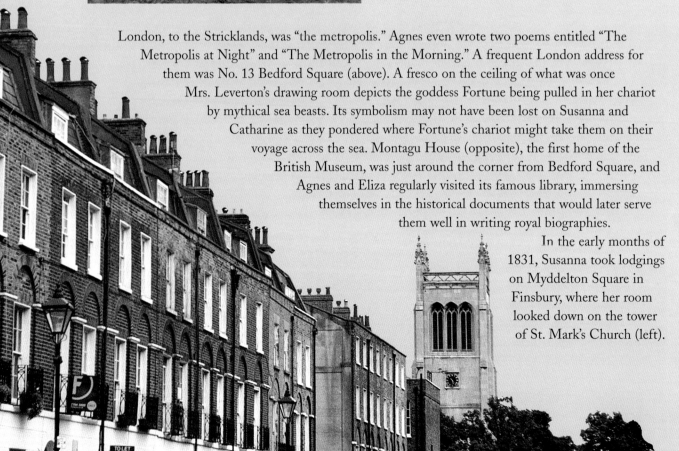

London, to the Stricklands, was "the metropolis." Agnes even wrote two poems entitled "The Metropolis at Night" and "The Metropolis in the Morning." A frequent London address for them was No. 13 Bedford Square (above). A fresco on the ceiling of what was once Mrs. Leverton's drawing room depicts the goddess Fortune being pulled in her chariot by mythical sea beasts. Its symbolism may not have been lost on Susanna and Catharine as they pondered where Fortune's chariot might take them on their voyage across the sea. Montagu House (opposite), the first home of the British Museum, was just around the corner from Bedford Square, and Agnes and Eliza regularly visited its famous library, immersing themselves in the historical documents that would later serve them well in writing royal biographies.

In the early months of 1831, Susanna took lodgings on Myddelton Square in Finsbury, where her room looked down on the tower of St. Mark's Church (left).

CHAPTER THREE

Courtship and Marriage

WHEN JOHN DUNBAR MOODIE RETURNED TO Britain from South Africa in 1830, he had two purposes in mind. The first was to find a publisher for a book he planned to write about his eleven years in the Cape Colony. The second was to woo a wife and companion who, he hoped, would be willing to return there with him. He was a pensioned soldier and an established farmer who was now eager to terminate his bachelorhood. Naturally, London drew him like a magnet. There he renewed acquaintances with his old Cape Town friends the Pringles, and while visiting their home was introduced to another houseguest, Miss Susanna Strickland. The two were soon involved in a whirlwind courtship that was both intensely passionate and fraught with challenges.

Certainly, the moment was right for these two

"Ye are wither'd, sweet buds! but love's hand can pourtray,
    On Memory's tablets, each delicate hue,
And recall to my bosom the long happy day,
    When he gathered ye, fresh sprinkled over with dew.
Ah, never did garland so lovely appear,
    For his warm lip had breath'd on each beautiful flower,
And the pearl on each leaf was less bright than the tear,
    That gleam'd in his eyes, in that rapturous hour."

— from "Lines on a Bunch of Withered Flowers,
Gathered on Hampstead Heath," written by Susanna after a
walk with John Moodie on the Heath (below).

youthful spirits. At thirty-three, John had been a soldier in the Napoleonic Wars, had seen something of the world and had developed a property he could call his own: a farm in South Africa's Groote Valley. Susanna was twenty-seven and, though torn between possibilities available to her, did not wish to face the long and lonely corridor of a spinster's life. In John she found an adventurer and a soldier who was also warm-hearted, generous and of a decidedly literary bent. In Susanna, John found a lively young woman who was caught up in many of the social issues of the day and eager to develop her literary potential. Though they both had experienced earlier passions and disappointments, they saw themselves as fellow romantics, happily brought together by friendly circumstance.

It was a love match, but neither had financial means beyond their own earning power, and there were few possibilities of inheritance or family support. John had his half-pay military pension, but his South African property had little current cash value despite the work he had put into it. If they were to marry, what could they do to support themselves and their offspring? A married couple needed an income of about £1,000 per year to meet living expenses. Literary income, they knew, could not sustain them.

Therefore, in the summer of 1830, just two months into their relationship, John sailed north to his boyhood home in the Orkneys to revisit family connections and to sniff out financial prospects while Susanna returned to Reydon. In a letter to his dear "Susie" dated August 19, 1830, he describes sailing past Southwold in a fog, where "perhaps my dear girl was walking on the beach."

I felt as if my heart could have leaped ashore and taken up its abode with yours for ever — Ah! would to God this wretched corporeal frame … were as free and insubstantial as my Spirit: — how delighted and swiftly would it fly to the arms of my beloved Susie — to bask in her sunny smiles, what countless kisses would I imprint on her dear lips — kind heaven … give me only her I love; I ask no more for this world to make me happy!

Revisiting Melsetter, the old Moodie manor house on the island of Hoy where he was born, John was filled with nostalgia for a time when his family controlled this large Orkney estate and its tenant farms. But such ownership had long since passed from them and, as the fourth son of a once-distinguished family, he had nothing to hope for from that source. Still, he sought out relatives and old friends in search of prospects.

In his absence, while she waited for his letters, Susanna found herself experiencing second thoughts about the marriage. Back in Suffolk she was once again exposed to the strong influence of her Congregationalist friends. Having converted the spring before she met her soldier-lover, she was still acutely conscious of the personal commitment she had entered into just months earlier. The architect of her conversion had been James Ritchie, the pastor of the small Congregational gathering in the nearby village of Wrentham. Ritchie had no interest in allowing his convert to escape easily, and he urged her to follow the call of the spirit over that of the flesh. His persuasions as well as

The Congregational chapel at Wrentham (above and below) was a plain, modest building, and Susanna's attendance there appalled her mother and sisters. To them, as Catharine later wrote, it "bordered on heresy." To make matters worse, Susanna also made her conversion to Nonconformist religion very public in *Enthusiasm, and Other Poems*, in which she praised the simple faith of "the unlearned and those of low estate."

ENTHUSIASM.

OH for the spirit which inspired of old
The seer's prophetic song—the voice that spake
Through Israel's warrior king.   The strains that burst
In thrilling tones from Zion's heaven-strung harp,
Float down the tide of ages, shedding light
On pagan shores and nations far remote :
Eternal as the God they celebrate,
Their fame shall last when Time's long race is run,
And yon refulgent eye of this fair world,—
Its light and centre,—into darkness shrinks,
Eclipsed for ever by the glance of Him
Whose rising sheds abroad eternal day.

B

A Bloomsbury Wedding

Despite Susanna's Congregational "enthusiasm," her marriage to John Moodie was blessed by the Church of England. It was a fairly simple occasion, no doubt concluded by the signing of the register as depicted in the period painting above. The setting was the handsome new St. Pancras Church, built in the fashionable neo-classical style with a columned tower (opposite) and faced with white Portland stone that has since darkened from years of London smoke. On each side of the church stands a caryatid porch (left), inspired by the Temple of the Erectheum on the Acropolis.

Susanna's mounting fears about South Africa, a place she associated with dangerous wild animals and slavery, led her to write to John in Scotland, breaking off the engagement. Once he returned to London, however, John talked through her hopes and needs, until she finally agreed to marry him. As Catharine watched the dramatic events unfolding in her sister's life, she found a gentle humour in Susanna's dilemma; it spoke to her of "the vagaries of woman-kind." Eight months later, on the occasion of Susanna and John's marriage, she wrote, "In spite of the warning of her good padre and her Southwold friends to love none other than a good man of their church, poor Susie has become a convert to Lieut. Dunbar Moodie."

Catharine served as Susanna's bridesmaid, the only sister to attend the London wedding on April 4, 1831. Mrs. Strickland refused to make such a long journey, even though this wedding was the first among her brood. The ceremony took place at St. Pancras Church, Euston, in north Bloomsbury. The Pringles hosted the wedding breakfast, Papa Pringle gave Susanna away and Thomas Cheesman entertained the wedding party in Newman Street after the ceremony. Mary Prince — or "Black Mary," as Susanna affectionately called her — also attended, wearing a new outfit for the occasion. Catharine detected a sadness in her sister's demeanour, but if there were concerns in Susanna's heart, they were more likely for the apparent betrayal of her Congregationalist commitment than any misgivings about her partner.

The newlyweds stayed in London for a few weeks but then, mindful of expenses, they moved back to Suffolk, renting a cottage near the sea at Southwold, within comfortable walking distance of Reydon Hall. In marriage, Susanna was "so very happy" that she doubted "such cannot long exist on earth." To Emma Bird she reported rapturously,

Ah, he is so kind, so good, so indulgent to all my wayward fits, that I look up to him as my guardian Angel. I seem to lose my own identity in him, and become indifferent to every thing else in the world. "Ah," you will say, this is preaching like a young wife, wait a few years, and then tell me what you think of matrimony. I do not much fear the trial, my heart will never grow old or cold to him.

John Moodie quickly proved a popular addition to the Strickland family. Mrs. Strickland approved of his background and high moral character. Agnes was especially fond of "the Captain" and kept up a lively correspondence with him once the Moodies emigrated. Catharine regarded him as an excellent partner for her sister: "I would not exchange my worthy brother-in-law for any woman's brother-in-law that you can name," she told James Bird. "I feel assured that they stand as good a chance for domestic happiness as any two persons I know of."

At this time, Catharine's own chance for domestic happiness was undergoing severe strain. In the late 1820s she had become engaged to Thomas Harral's son Francis, even though the two had few resources to support their prospective marriage. But now the Harral household was in turmoil after the death of Francis's sister, Anna Laura. Thomas Harral's finances had arrived at a precarious point, and his second wife was behaving in strange and aggressive ways towards the Strickland girls. To deal with Francis's prolonged silence and the growing uncertainty of their engagement, Catharine went down to London early in 1831. While the Moodies honeymooned in a rented flat in Pentonville, Catharine accepted the hospitality of both Rebecca Leverton and her cousin Thomas Cheesman. She dined with her fiancé in Newman Street and sought to raise his sagging morale. Because of his father's financial difficulties, Francis had had to abandon his plans for a medical education. As he cast about for other opportunities, he was "out of spirits" and still struggling to find some way to live up to his commitment to his betrothed. "Perhaps," wrote Catharine, "the recent marriage of Susanna might contribute to depress him as his own prospects must seem darker when contrasted with those of Mr. Moodie."

Determination and focus were among Catharine's many strengths. Francis "is all the world to me," she told the Birds in a letter. Her strong resolution, however, was no match for circumstance. The second Mrs. Harral

mischievously planted a false wedding announcement in a London newspaper, as if to mock the pretenses of her stepson and the country girl who claimed him. "I abhor her character," wrote Catharine, "and I hold her malicious conduct in detestation." Crumbling under the weight of his situation, Francis was grateful to accept Catharine's offer to release him from his bond. Without further ado, he left for Dorset to take up an apprenticeship to a pharmacist, leaving his former fiancée to deal with her loss as best she could.

Deeply disappointed but characteristically realistic, Catharine found a sympathetic companion and generous friend in her "Aunt Rebecca." To take Catharine's mind off her troubles, Mrs. Leverton encouraged her to stay with her and enjoy the pleasures of exploring London and meeting new friends. "[She] is very kind to me and treats me with the greatest confidence as a friend and a child at the same time," Catharine reported. She proved such an agreeable companion that Mrs. Leverton invited Catharine to travel with her over the summer, autumn and winter of 1831–32. Catharine accompanied her aunt to the Leverton estate at Waltham Cross in Hertfordshire, and then continued on with her to Oxford, Cheltenham and Bath. During this happy sojourn, news reached her that the Moodies were seriously contemplating emigration to Canada in the spring of 1832. Declaring her resolve to be home at Reydon in March, she wrote at year's end, "I could not endure the thought of parting from [Susanna] at a distance and possibly for years, perhaps for life."

A refreshed and well-travelled Catharine came home to find the Moodies enjoying their Southwold cottage and delving deeply into their astonishing plans. She learned that they had received a friendly visit during the winter from Robert Reid, the father-in-law of their beloved younger brother, Samuel. Reid had moved to Upper Canada from Ireland in 1822 with his brother-in-law Thomas A. Stewart to develop a large land grant in Douro Township, forty miles north of Lake Ontario. His family's success story and his sensible encouragement found an echo in the salesmanship of William Cattermole, an emigration agent for the Canada Company who was recruiting in Suffolk during that winter. John attended one of his lectures in Yoxford, purchased his pamphlet and heard more of what the Canadian colony offered someone like himself.

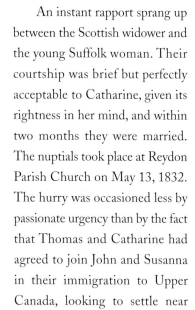

Thomas Traill

At the Moodies' cottage, Catharine encountered two delightful surprises. The first was that her new niece, Catherine Mary, bore her name. The other was a houseguest of the Moodies, a friend and fellow officer of John's named Thomas Traill. Like John, he was from the Orkneys, but his experiences of the world had been much different. Thomas Traill was a thirty-nine-year-old widower who had lived for a decade on the continent with his wife, Anne Fotheringhame, and their two young sons. When Anne died in 1828 of tuberculosis in Vevey, Switzerland, Thomas returned to Scotland to place his sons with his late wife's family. He then set out to renew old acquain-tances and investigate new prospects for himself. He was a cultivated and sensitive man of a sort that Catharine found engaging and attractive. He had attended Wadham College, Oxford, spoke five languages, read widely, enjoyed good conversation and had a breadth of cosmopolitan experience.

An instant rapport sprang up between the Scottish widower and the young Suffolk woman. Their courtship was brief but perfectly acceptable to Catharine, given its rightness in her mind, and within two months they were married. The nuptials took place at Reydon Parish Church on May 13, 1832. The hurry was occasioned less by passionate urgency than by the fact that Thomas and Catharine had agreed to join John and Susanna in their immigration to Upper Canada, looking to settle near brother Sam in Douro Township. By the date of the wedding, all the essential plans were in place.

At Reydon, there was quiet dissatisfaction. Mrs. Strickland was deeply saddened at the thought of losing not one but two of her daughters to the New World. Several of the sisters, notably the strong-minded Agnes, thought Catharine's match unsatisfactory on several grounds. Indelicate haste was one thing, but here was a widower with two teenage children, a man without many prospects or evident energy. Agnes felt that Catharine would be far wiser to wait for an elderly but rich suitor — her own unhurried

strategy. However, there was no stopping Catharine once her mind was made up. Writing to the Birds on her wedding day, she made it clear that "she [was] willing to lose all for the sake of one dear valued friend and husband to share with him all the changes and chances of a settler's life."

Two days after their wedding, they were gone. Their haste was driven by several pressing matters — Thomas had to introduce his new wife to his family in Scotland and convey his plans to his first wife's family, who were looking after his sons, Walter (age seventeen) and John (thirteen). He also had to make financial arrangements to cover the costs of the passage and the expenses involved in setting up a home in Canada. And he had to find ways to provide for his sons during his absence; his great dream was that in a few years they would join him in Upper Canada.

Thomas was well aware that, unlike his friend John Moodie, he lacked the experience and youthful energy to be an effective farmer on his own.

Catharine looked forward to the excitement of both her first visit to Scotland and a new life in Canada. In her 1826 book *The Young Emigrants*, she had envisioned that there was so much to be discovered in the New World that one could never tire of the experience. Yet the enormity of what they were about to do must have come home to both sisters on May 15 as they tearfully embraced on a Southwold beach beside a rowboat that would take the Traills out to the coastal steamer the *City of London*. As Catharine had written in an affectionate farewell letter to James Bird, she was fully aware that "the waves of the Atlantic will soon roll between her and all the friends of her youth."

The nave of St. Margaret's Parish Church in Reydon (left) was the scene of the May 13, 1832, wedding of Catharine Parr Strickland to Thomas Traill. Only two days later they boarded a coastal steamer for the first leg of their journey to Canada.

CHAPTER FOUR

The Voyage Out

A stormy sea, like the one depicted in this 1822 engraving of Southwold harbour,
delayed the Moodies' departure for Canada in May of 1832.

FOR THE MOODIES, LEAVING WAS A CHAOTIC AND dramatic business — so many matters had to be arranged, so many items carefully packed, so many good-byes said and tears shed. Susanna hid her fears as best she could. Canada was, by many reports, a cold, hard and daunting country fraught with dangers. Reports of cholera at British seaports only added to her anxiety. A few days after the Traills' departure, as several friends gathered on the Southwold beach to see them off, their frustrations began. A storm delayed their initial attempt to depart; indeed, it was two days later, on their third attempt that the local pilot boat was able to deliver them to the *City of Edinburgh*, destined for Leith, Edinburgh's seaport. Their party, which included Susanna's servant, Hannah, and James Bird, the eleven-year-old son of James and Emma Bird, was to connect there with the transatlantic ship on which they had booked

(Above) Edinburgh's port of Leith as the Moodies saw it, and (below) as it appears today.

their passage. But on account of the delay, they missed their connection and were forced to seek out entirely new arrangements for the Atlantic crossing.

During their hiatus, Susanna was torn between anxiety and fascination. Edinburgh stimulated her immensely — there was so much to see and explore. With young James Bird, she climbed up to admire the view from Arthur's Seat. In terms of "romantic sublimity," the city had "no equal in the wide world." As a country, Scotland lived up to its reputation as "the land of poetry and romance," and she was pleased by the hospitality they received and the broad accents she heard. However, she could not help but feel that the delays were "bad omen[s]," foreboding "evil" for their future. She had been heartened by the words of the captain of the *City of Edinburgh* as their ship approached the city. "[T]he rock-defended fortress of Quebec," he told her, would provide her with almost as fine a view as Edinburgh. In her autobiographical novel *Flora Lyndsay*, she recounted her reply: "I have contemplated a residence in Canada with feelings of such antipathy, that your description of Quebec almost reconciles me to my lot. I can never hate a country which abounds in natural beauty."

For nearly a month, the Moodies waited in Leith. John booked passage on a ship named the *Flora* but became uneasy about conditions on board when he had the opportunity to inspect the ship. Then Susanna spotted a posting for another brig called the *Anne*, which announced it would sail for Canada on July 1, two weeks later than the *Flora*. Although it promised more comfortable accommodations for cabin passengers, the further delay worried John as he realized that newcomers needed as much time as possible in Canada before the onset of winter.

In Edinburgh, Susanna climbed up the craggy slopes of Arthur's Seat (below, at left) for a view of "Auld Reekie," as the smoky city was known. (Above) The view of Edinburgh Castle has changed little since the 1830s.

In the end the *Anne* won their approval, in part because the *Flora*'s captain proved a nasty negotiator. By contrast, the captain of the *Anne*, a "rough, blunt looking tar" named George Rodgers, promised them special advantages, including the small "state-cabin" for Susanna. There would be seventy-two passengers in steerage, but the Moodie party would have the run of the upper deck. With rumours of cholera growing by the day, and with Susanna briefly taken ill, they nevertheless had to be ready to embark immediately upon the captain's announcement. This time, without friends to cheer them and in a gloomy downpour, they boarded their ship and set sail into the Firth of Forth on July 1, 1832.

Catharine's Scottish travels were more extensive. With Thomas she spent the better part of two months visiting Edinburgh, the Highlands and the Orkneys, meeting friends of Thomas and family members, including his father, the Presbyterian minister on the island of Sanday. There she visited Westove, the Traill

EDINBURGH.

In *Flora Lyndsay*, Susanna describes John pointing out the famous rock formation on the island of Hoy (above, at left) and his boyhood home of Melsetter (above, at right) as their ship passes the Orkneys.(Below) A view of Sanday, where Thomas Traill's family lived.

"That giant hill that looks like an old man
in a highland bonnet— that is the old man of Hoy.
That old house is M__,
where I was born and brought up."

family home on the island's northern peninsula. An extensive and impressive manor house, it dated from the seventeenth century. At Kirkwall, she was also welcomed by relatives and found special fascination in the rocky terrain and hardy fauna of the famous islands. Her sunny disposition and warm affection for Thomas impressed those she met.

Thomas, however, had told Catharine very little about the actual state of his patrimony. The cruel truth was that Westove was a much-encumbered estate, one that produced too little income to meet the debts placed against it. Thomas was guaranteed a yearly income of £100, but it was evident that nothing more could be expected in the foreseeable future. To arrange for the money that would allow his wife a relatively comfortable passage to Canada and provide for their life there, a loan was the only answer, even though he had already accumulated a debt of £300 during his first wife's long illness. Nonetheless, he contracted with an Edinburgh bank for a new loan of £200 and turned his attention to their immediate plans.

With money now in hand, there was an urgent need to book their passage. After some frustrating delays, Thomas finally managed to reserve two places at £15 each on the *Rowley*, a fast-sailing brig preparing to leave from Greenock on July 7. With no time to spare, they had to make their way southward, even though Catharine had fallen ill. When they reached Greenock, she was still so unwell that she had to be carried on board. Both the captain and steward expressed concern about her health and even her ability to survive the crossing. The *Rowley* made good headway down the Clyde, skirted the Hebrides and, carrying no steerage passengers and only four paying customers on deck, it made the Atlantic crossing in just over five weeks. So swift was the voyage that, although the Traills left Scotland a week later than the Moodies, they arrived in Quebec on August 18, nearly two weeks before the *Anne*. Fortunately, Catharine, who was the only woman aboard, recovered her health after departure and was able to endure the monotony of the crossing with only occasional bouts of seasickness. She pitied her husband as he wearily paced the deck with "nothing to see, nothing to hear, nothing to do, and nothing to read." A woman at least could sew and knit in her captivity. With each day a sad echo of the one before, Thomas seemed "a very pitiable creature." In making such observations, Catharine was perhaps beginning to discover how quiet and withdrawn her husband could be in uncongenial circumstances. When his depressive nature asserted itself, it could be both formidable and debilitating.

Passing Newfoundland, the *Rowley* entered the

Cabin passengers taking lunch
on the forecastle deck.

Bic Island, off Rimouski, Quebec, was for many years a pilot station in the St. Lawrence.

At Quebec, neither Catharine nor Susanna went ashore because of the threat of cholera.
But both of them admired the view from the river, and Susanna later exulted, "Canadians, rejoice in your beautiful city!
Rejoice and be worthy of her, for few, very few of the sons of men can point to such a spot as Quebec."

mouth of the St. Lawrence River. At Bic Island the ship anchored to await a pilot, and Thomas went ashore with the captain. He returned with a bouquet of wildflowers that cheered Catharine immensely as she identified the species and luxuriated in the perfumes of earth and shore. Here, as at other stops, she was confined to the deck. At Grosse Ile, "a beautiful rocky island" where the *Rowley* had to dock for three days for a mandatory inspection for cholera and other contagious illnesses, she could only wait and bemoan her continuing imprisonment. "Nothing," she wrote, "can exceed the longing desire I feel to be allowed to land and explore this picturesque island; the weather is so fine, and the waving groves of green, the little rocky bays and inlets of the island, appear so tempting; but to all my entreaties the visiting surgeon who came on board returned a decided negative."

At Quebec City she was not allowed ashore either, and was therefore unable to climb to the fortress atop the old city. Instead, she wrote with muted regret:

Nothing can be more imposing than the situation of Quebec, built on the sides and summit of a magnificent rock.... I did, indeed, regret the loss of this noble prospect, the equal of which I suppose I shall never see. It would have been something to have thought on and recalled in after years, when buried in the solitude of the Canadian woods.

She did not, however, allow her confinement on board to limit her observations or her judgements. The rocky riverbanks and the "white cottages, gardens and hanging orchards" caught her attention, as did "the horse ferry-boats" that ran between Quebec and the town of Lévis on the south shore. But, as she expressed in a letter to her mother and sisters, "much less is done with this romantic situation than might be effected if good taste were exercised in the buildings.... Nature here has done all, and man but little, excepting sticking up some ugly wooden cottages, as mean as they are tasteless."

Having passed Quebec with as much haste as possible, the *Rowley* was towed to Montreal by steamer, arriving on August 17. Here, at last, both Traills were able to debark, having reached their ticketed destination. But to them Montreal was "the city of the pestilence," marked by its open sewers and the many signs of illness and grieving they saw in the streets. Cholera seemed to be everywhere and on everyone's mind. To make matters worse, the weather was uncomfortably hot and humid. Relieved as she was to be ashore at last, Catharine was plunged into melancholy as she considered the plight of many of the new immigrants. She heard reports of whole families having been killed by the disease, and she grieved for those "driven by the stern hand of necessity from his country and home, perhaps to be overtaken by sickness or want in a land of strangers."

But all was not gloomy for those who could afford refuge. The Traills found comfortable rooms and good food at the Nelson Hotel, where they met numerous people of interest, chiefly middle-class immigrants like themselves. In her limited rambles, Catharine was delighted to observe the new Catholic basilica, Notre Dame, which was still under construction, and she admired the charming scenery of the city, including the mountain that loomed above the hotel.

Still, there were unforeseen delays. Their luggage was held up in customs for a couple of days. Then, just when they were ready to depart for Lachine, Catharine became violently ill with symptoms that were consistent with those of cholera. Forced to her bed, she endured several days of severe pain, although ably nursed by the sister of the landlord and the vigilant care of a Montreal doctor. In her own accounts she makes no connection between the illness she suffered in Scotland prior to boarding the ship and the one necessitating her Montreal confinement — it is possible that she brought cholera with her from Scotland. Whatever the case, after four days of acute suffering, she was deemed able to carry on westward, even though she was still too weak to proceed under her own power.

For the Moodies, meanwhile, the mere matter of getting to Canada was fraught with difficulty and anxiety. The *Anne* was becalmed off the Grand Banks for nearly two weeks, during which food and fresh water supplies ran low, necessitating strict rationing. Susanna became so ill that she had to wean Katie, since a diet of oatmeal and spoonfuls of port were hardly sustaining for a nursing mother. At the same time, tensions developed among the cabin passengers. Susanna's maid-servant, Hannah, engaged in a disturbing flirtation with Captain Rodgers and became more rebellious as the trip continued, virtually withdrawing her services as Katie's nursemaid as they neared Canada.

Eight weeks at sea proved a cruel test for all on

board. It was the 25th of August before they reached Cape Rosier and were able to take on fresh water and supplies. Refortified, Susanna's excitement rose as the ship advanced up the river. She was thrilled by the mountainous grandeur of the landscape before her, especially on the north shore.

From the deck of the *Anne*, Susanna had to wait patiently while the medical authorities at the quarantine station on Grosse Ile examined the surviving steerage passengers. As a cabin passenger, she was only required to send Hannah on shore to wash their clothing and bedding. Prevented, as Catharine had been, from going ashore, Susanna had plenty of time to observe the large number of poor immigrants whose ships were also at anchor for medical inspection. What she saw was a pandemonium that appalled her. Unlike the distant mountains, which aroused both her aesthetic fascination and inner fear, these "vicious, uneducated barbarians who form the surplus of the over-populous European countries" evoked only disgust in her. Susanna's descriptions of the poor Irish have left her susceptible to charges of English superiority and insensitivity ever since.

For her, Grosse Ile provided a first, hard lesson about experience and expectation in Canada. As Captain Rodgers said to her on deck, "many things look well at a distance which are bad enough when near." The pattern would be repeated at stop after stop as the Moodies proceeded westward towards Upper

This 1843 watercolour of Notre Dame Street in Montreal by John Murray shows the Catholic basilica that was still under construction when seen by Catharine in 1832. She admired the interior, however, particularly the large window behind the altar and "the extreme lightness of the architecture."

"The river-side portion of the town is entirely mercantile. Its narrow, dirty streets and dark houses, with heavy iron shutters, have a disagreeable appearance, which cannot but make an unfavourable impression on the mind of a British traveller."

— Catharine Parr Traill, *The Backwoods of Canada*

Canada and their new home. Whatever aspects of natural beauty she was able to observe at a distance were counterbalanced by an intrusion of disturbing human activity, perpetrated by the type of people she would usually have been able to avoid were she still in England. While the beauty of the fortress at Quebec stirred her deeply, Susanna grew increasingly alarmed at what seemed a world of misrule and death around her. Up close, the city was "a filthy hole." The bells tolled steadily, announcing death after death from the dreaded cholera. Repulsed by what she saw and heard, she began feeling "a hatred so intense [for Canada] that I longed to die."

With each experience, her hostility and disorientation sharpened. When the *Anne* was in a collision with another ship, the *Horsley Hill*, in the harbour, she was asked by the captain to help calm the women in steerage. Drawing on "a sort of nerving of the spirit," she tried to restore order among the terrified women. For her efforts — heroic under the circumstances, or so she imagined — she was sworn at and brushed aside. Pleading with the "headstrong creatures" to be patient and to trust in the British crew, her words went unheeded. "I might as well have preached to the winds," she recalled.

Most of the steerage passengers left the ship at Quebec. Then the *Anne*, like Catharine's *Rowley*, was towed to Montreal by a steamer. As they proceeded up the St. Lawrence, Susanna continued to feel "sad forebodings," which she later knew to have been "too prophetic of the future." Of her brief experience of Montreal, she had little to say in *Roughing It in the Bush*. The city seemed to her much as her sister had described Quebec — "dirty and ill-paved," with open sewers that "loaded the air with intolerable effluvia." On the day of their arrival they were transfixed and then horrified by another dark event. From the deck of the *Anne* she witnessed the drowning of a sailor in the harbour. No one came to his aid after he fell overboard, and when help did come it was too late. She found herself gazing, "half-maddened by excitement, on the fearful spectacle." While she used the drama to pass judgement on "the barbarous indifference" of men towards their fellows, what may strike the reader about her description is the naked honesty of her own reactions. Death was imposing itself upon her view of Canadian experience. It seemed to be everywhere, and the spectacle of it thrilled her in spite of herself.

Much concerned about the cholera epidemic, the Moodies made their stay in Montreal as short as possible, allowing for the fact that they had to submit to the required customs inspection. At first, the ship was their "ark of safety" in the plague-infected city, but when the disease was discovered on board they hurriedly shifted to Goodenough's Hotel, where they enjoyed a brief night of what seemed luxurious accommodation before they boarded a stagecoach for Lachine.

Ahead lay Upper Canada and, for Susanna, still greater fears.

William Workman's 1840 depiction of the foot of Jacques Cartier Square does not show the open sewers described by Susanna during the height of the cholera plague in Montreal eight years before.

A Visit to Grosse Ile

"The dreadful cholera was depopulating Quebec and Montreal when our ship cast anchor off Grosse Isle, [sic] on the 30th of August, 1832...." So begins the first chapter of *Roughing It in the Bush*. A small island thirty-three miles downstream from Quebec, Grosse Ile had been selected as an immigration quarantine station only months before the Moodies' arrival. A European cholera pandemic had struck England in 1831–32 during a time of great emigration, when an average of 30,000 immigrants, two-thirds of them from Ireland, were arriving annually in Quebec. The colonial authorities had decreed that all arriving steerage passengers must disembark at Grosse Ile and be inspected there. The sick were herded into makeshift sheds where most of them died.

For cabin passengers like the Moodies and the Traills no inspection was required, though, ironically, Catharine may well have been carrying the cholera virus. She noted that one of the other passenger ships anchored off Grosse Ile was flying a yellow flag, "the melancholy symbol of disease." Catharine longed to explore the picturesque rocky island but had to content herself with a basket of raspberries, strawberries and wildflowers brought to her by the ship's surgeon. She observed the steerage passengers washing their clothes onshore and the children "pursuing each other in wanton glee rejoicing in their newly-acquired liberty." To her sister Susanna, who insisted on going ashore, this same scene was a seething mass of shrieking, dirty, half-naked people. She describes how she "shrank, with feelings almost akin to fear, from the hard-featured, sun-burnt harpies, as they elbowed rudely past me." She was particularly horrified by one unclothed Irishman who waved his shillelagh and shouted, "Whurrah! my boys! Shure we'll all be jintlemen!" She concluded her chapter by noting ruefully, "Thus ended my first day's experience of the land of all our hopes."

Today, a Celtic cross stands on Grosse Ile (left) to commemorate the more than 6,000 Irish immigrants whose dreams for the New World ended there. Most of them were felled by the deadly typhus epidemic of 1847–48, which occurred as record numbers of immigrants (above, bottom) fled the terrible potato famine (above, top) in Ireland. Grosse Ile would remain an immigration quarantine station until 1937.

Grosse Ile (above) is now a national park where visitors can tour the buildings preserved from the island's time as a quarantine station and an important entry point into North America for thousands of immigrants. One of the most poignant sites is the Irish cemetery (below), where coffins were stacked three deep in long trenches during the 1847 typhus epidemic.

CHAPTER FIVE

"Our First Settlement"

THE MOODIES AND THE TRAILLS ARRIVED IN Cobourg, Upper Canada, within two weeks of each other in the late summer of 1832. For Catharine, the trip was a difficult one, given her weakened state, but she carried on gamely. What she was able to observe from the stagecoach and from the boat deck left her more impressed by the progress of civilization in Lower Canada than in the upper province. She found the "rocky and picturesque aspect" of the Thousand Islands appealing, but she regretted that their ship passed the town of Kingston, which she called "the key to the lakes," in darkness.

For the Traills, Cobourg was but a brief overnight stop. Peterborough and Lakefield lay to the north, and the couple were bent upon getting there as soon as they could make travel arrangements. They were eager to meet with Sam Strickland, whom Catharine had not seen in seven years, and to begin the process of getting settled on their land grant before the arrival of winter. Despite the uncomfortable trip from Montreal, Catharine's health had improved considerably, and there was little now to hold them back. They heard warnings from experienced settlers that they would face only problems and disappointments ahead, but Catharine, as was her nature, opted to look on the bright side.

At that time, Cobourg was nearly as important a stopping-off point for immigrants as the town of York (which became Toronto in 1834). Catharine remarked favourably upon the "neatly built and flourishing village [of Cobourg, which had] many good stores, mills, a banking-house, printing-office, where a newspaper is published once a week." The Cobourg *Star*, under the editorship of R.D. Chatterton, an English-born journalist, was at that time the only paper published in Upper Canada between York and Kingston. Its Anglo-conservative outlook appealed to Catharine, as did the pleasing look of "a very pretty church."[1]

"A neatly built and flourishing village" is Catharine's description of Cobourg, and this 1840 watercolour by Philip Bainbrigge confirms that impression. She would not have seen the white columned Victoria College depicted at left, as it was not opened until 1838. The building still stands in Cobourg today (opposite).

View near the Head of the River Sᵗ. Lawrence, Canada
Fort Henry and Kingston in the distance

Two 1830 watercolours by Captain Thomas Burrowes depict the St. Lawrence near Kingston (above) and the Thousand Islands (right). Burrowes was employed in the construction and maintenance of the Rideau Canal and created 114 watercolours of eastern Ontario between 1826 and 1846.

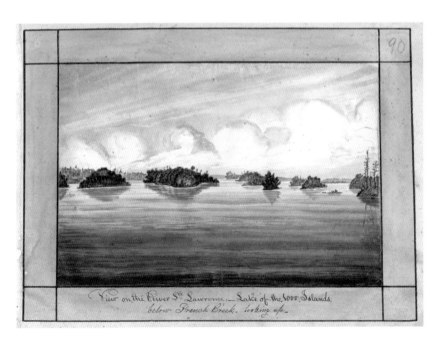

View on the River Sᵗ. Lawrence — Lake of the 1000 Islands, below French Creek. looking up.

Just as noteworthy to Catharine was evidence in the village of "a select society," for she reported to her mother that "many families of respectability ha[d] fixed their residences in or near the town." Catharine was always cheered by indications of an established English social presence. That she was now the wife of a British officer had become her most important calling card; it was how she would choose to identify herself in *The Backwoods of Canada*, the book she would begin to write two years later.

The Moodies arrived in Cobourg late in the evening of September 9. Susanna felt much relieved to be there, for they had been dodging the "phantom" of cholera all the way from Montreal and she had experienced a number of violations of her much-valued privacy. Like Catharine, she had experienced moments of curt and ungracious service in her travels westward but, unlike her sister, she took delight in later transforming certain encounters into comic vignettes, using her ear for vernacular voices and her eye for telling physical appearances.[2]

Storms and night travel prevented Susanna from seeing both the Thousand Islands and Kingston as their steamship, the *William IV*, followed the north shore of Lake Ontario. For most of their night on the lake they were kept awake by "the uproarious conduct of a wild Irish emigrant" who, deep in drink, sang loudly and harangued other passengers about Irish politics outside their cabin doors. It was a tired group of travellers that arrived at Cobourg the next night, only to learn that, because there were so many immigrants present in town, there were no available rooms anywhere. While John was desperately canvassing for accommodation, Susanna recognized a familiar face among the clientele of Oren Strong's Hotel. Tom Wales, a young man from Southwold who had attended Cattermole's lecture in Suffolk with John and immigrated to Douro Township in May, generously offered his own bed to Susanna and Katie for the night.

Tom (who would become Tom Wilson in *Roughing It in the Bush*) was consumed with disgust for "this confounded country." His tale was a litany of negatives — cheating land dealers, mosquitoes and black flies, awful food, illnesses like the ague (from which he was currently shaking and suffering), lack of privacy, mud holes and corduroy roads and deadly isolation. Wales claimed that his only Canadian friend was the bedraggled bear now tethered outside the hotel. He had returned to Cobourg to book a ship home to Suffolk before the winter set in. Good riddance to Canada, was his manic song.

"Good heavens," said Susanna, "let us never go to the woods!" Her trepidations echoed John's current thinking. If they could afford to buy a cleared or partially cleared property close to Lake Ontario, he thought they would be far better off than if they tried to start a farm from scratch on wild land. From his South African experience, John knew what it took to develop a farm in a new and unfamiliar place. They would be better off closer to amenities — and to the kind of like-minded, genteel families with whom they could comfortably socialize. Confirmed in this plan, John spent many days investigating possible farms with a prosperous settler he had met, and then with a "land-jobber" named Charles Clark (the C__ of *Roughing It in the Bush*) who ran a general store in Cobourg.

Though John had £300 to work with, he found most available properties in the area beyond his means. But, as autumn was about to begin, he knew that he was pressed for time. A shrewd operator, Clark gauged his client well. He saw in Moodie a likely prospect to buy a good farm in a difficult and unattractive situation, one currently dominated by a nest of Yankee farmers and squatters whom he deemed uncouth and unruly. Clark's plan was to force them out of the area, and he sensed that he could appeal to John Moodie to be part of the vanguard for this "clean-up" campaign.

The farm that Moodie purchased was located in Hamilton Township, on Gage's Creek some eight miles from Cobourg and four miles from Port Hope. Its owner was Joe Harris (the Old Joe H__ of *Roughing It in the Bush*), the son of a "late Loyalist" family who had moved north in the 1790s. Harris had fallen deeply in debt to Charles Clark and was willing to sell his land, but only under certain favourable terms. His primary condition was that he not be required to leave the farmhouse until the winter snow fell. His wife was pregnant and could not be moved until the ground was frozen and thereby suited for travel. Naively, Moodie accepted the deal. Although they now owned a cleared, two-hundred-acre farm of gently rolling hills that they called Melsetter after John's birthplace, they were forced to set up camp on a nearby property in a dilapidated cabin. Susanna was shocked when she saw the "miserable hut … not a house, but a cattle-shed, or pig-sty" in which they would have to live. Cobourg, which she had found thin in terms of culture and society, must have seemed a paradise when compared to Gage's Creek. Susanna did her best to make the space livable for John, herself and baby Katie, the disgruntled Hannah, and Tom Wales, who agreed to stay with them while he waited for a ship departing for England.

The "pig-sty" came courtesy of Charles Clark's arrangements, but he was soon negotiating to sell the property on which it stood to another immigrant. Within a month, the Moodies were forced to decamp. Clark's hasty solution was to negotiate a deal with Joe Harris's mother who, while at odds with her son and his wife, was living in a small cabin across the glen from the main farmhouse. The Moodies had to pay her to leave this cabin on their own property, then set up house again in restricted quarters. (At least, by this time, Tom Wales had left for England.) During the entire winter, Harris refused to leave the farmhouse, exercising a sort of "what-can-you-do-to-me" attitude that left the Moodies frustrated but uncertain where to turn.[3]

For all their careful budgeting and planning, John and Susanna (who was pregnant with their second child) had to endure the "iron winter of 1833" in close and cramped quarters, a few hundred yards from the much larger home they owned.[4] Joe Harris finally left for Gore's Landing on May 31, 1833. His parting shot was to leave a live skunk in a cupboard in the house. Over these months they also waved goodbye to Hannah, their unhappy English servant, and to a manservant named James. In their places the Moodies welcomed into their cramped household first Isabel (Bel) and then, in a driving snowstorm, the eccentric young Irishman John Monaghan, whose alleged "papist" history soon drove the Scottish-born Bel away.

For a year and a half the Moodies tried to farm Melsetter in Hamilton Township, and slowly they made progress, both in the quality of their living quarters and the operation of the farm. It was their hope that, with paid help, they might develop a life appropriate to their middle-class status, thereby having more leisure time to devote to their writing, social connections and business investments. As soon as they could manage, Susanna and John tried to place poetry and sketches with various Canadian and American newspapers and magazines. Both had works printed in the Cobourg *Star*, the New York *Albion* and some fledgling magazines in York in 1833. But Cobourg itself seemed hostile to literary endeavour. "We were reckoned no addition to the society," Susanna reported, as "authors and literary people [were] held in supreme detestation." She likely exaggerated the scorn she felt in being seen as a potential Mrs. Trollope, the visiting Englishwoman who had skewered Americans with her pen. She "tried to avoid all literary subjects" and to "conceal [her] bluestockings beneath the long conventional robes of the tamest common-place." Proudly she noted that she "could both make a shirt, and attend to the domestic arrangement of my family" as well as any of her female critics.

But with the farm now in their hands and the prospect of better neighbours being realized, they struck another bargain that resulted in a different set of problems. That spring, they entered into an agreement to work the land "on shares" with an English couple in the vicinity (named the O__'s by Susanna) who had presented themselves as experienced and willing partners. The Moodies hired them to undertake the lion's share

This colour sketch of a half-pay officer claiming his land is from a scrapbook kept by Lieutenant-Colonel Robert Brown, who had served with John Moodie in the Napoleonic wars and would later command the Northumberland militia. A depiction of a loyalist settler's first cabin is shown in a woodcut (below).

"The charred and blackened stumps on the few acres that had been cleared … were everything but picturesque" was Susanna's description of the land around the Traills' cabin in Douro. The stumps were a shock to her after the cleared fields of Hamilton Township.

of the work while they provided the seeds and equipment. That the agreement did not work out as they had hoped is an understatement that Susanna only partially disguises in her memoir.

In *Roughing It in the Bush*, mention of the O__'s might pass relatively unnoticed by the casual reader. Nor do historical documents reveal their actual identity, as they were not landowners in Hamilton Township at this time. Rather, they were clever opportunists who approached the Moodies at a susceptible moment — as they were preparing to move into their farmhouse and Susanna was enduring the final trimester of her pregnancy. The O__'s were, after all, English, and they were relatively presentable and experienced in farm work.

If one reads between the lines of Susanna's descriptions, it is clear that the O__'s quickly made life miserable for the Moodies in numerous ways.

In their farming and the harvesting of produce, they cheated their partners at every turn. Socially, Mrs. O__ presumed to a status she did not merit and gossiped freely about Susanna and her family. Thus, and perhaps surprisingly to readers of Susanna's book, it was the insufferable O__'s — and not the damn Yankees like Joe Harris — who finally drove the Moodies to sell their farm and head north to Douro. They felt trapped and hemmed in by an arrangement that disadvantaged and embarrassed them and compromised their much-valued privacy at every turn.

John Moodie was not a passive observer of the situation his family faced at Melsetter. He remained open-minded about other opportunities and twice made the long journey to Douro to visit Sam Strickland. While there, he weighed the merits of buying some adjacent land and moving north. Sam had already obtained some sixty-six acres for John in north Douro, along with other wild lands in Verulam and Fenelon townships, making up the four hundred acres to which John was entitled as a retired British officer. Before him, John had not only the stirring example of Sam's success since 1831 (he had cleared and planted twenty-five acres of land) but also Thomas Traill's rapid progress in clearing some of his land for planting. To have congenial family members as neighbours offered a welcome change, given what the Moodies were experiencing in Hamilton Township.

Though only forty miles separated the Moodies' first farm near Cobourg from the Traill homestead in Douro, getting from one to the other was an arduous journey of a day or more.

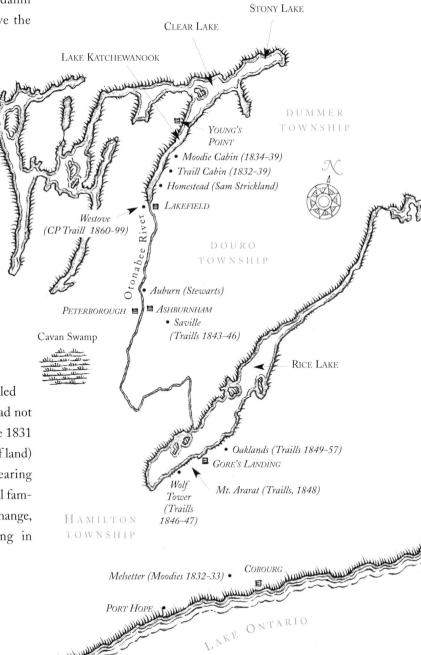

John talked enthusiastically with Sam about the idea of a development scheme to sell backwoods lands to prospective emigrants in Britain, among them some of John's Orkney friends and relatives. Sam's previous connection with the Canada Company, and his decade of experience in Upper Canada, would be their foundation. Towards the end of 1833, John made two purchases that brought his total Douro holdings to 360 acres. His property fronted on the east shore of Lake Katchewanook, about a mile north of the Traills' property and two miles north of Sam's homestead. The small village of Herriot's Falls (now Lakefield) was three miles to the south, adjacent to the point where Lake Katchewanook narrowed and rushed over a fifteen-foot waterfall into the swirling waters of the Otonabee River. Fresh signs of progress were evident. A bridge spanned the fast-flowing river, connecting Douro and Smith townships, and a small mill had been opened, thanks to the efforts of a young Scotsman named James Herriot whose name briefly attached itself to the small community.

With his new prospects, John Moodie was in a buoyant mood, and 1834 began as a very promising year. Maintaining his faith in the advice of Charles Clark, he decided to jump at what was called a surefire investment. It was a steamship named the *Cobourg*, which would soon ply the busy waters of Lake Ontario. To invest in the scheme, however, Moodie needed instant equity, so he decided to sell his half-pay military pension for 25 shares (at $25 each) in the steamboat. According to Clark, it was only a matter of time before the steamer began paying attractive dividends to its backers. But even as he entered into this invest-ment, John's attention was focused on the backwoods.[5] In the autumn of 1833, he arranged for a spacious log house to be constructed on his Douro property. Back in Hamilton Township, he put Melsetter up for sale and booked a livery firm to move his family north in February, once the roads were frozen and passable.

Catharine and Thomas Traill had had a much easier time settling in than the Moodies. After leaving Cobourg, they had travelled by stagecoach to Rice Lake, passing over the Rice Lake Plains that, Catharine was fascinated to learn, had been a traditional hunting ground of the Chippewa Indians. From a lakeside tavern on the south shore, they boarded a rather primitive steamer, the *Pem-o-dash* — or "Fireship," as the Natives called the first commercial boat to ply Rice Lake. It took them across the lake and up the Otonabee River to a point marked by impassable rapids, just below Peterborough.

After a long and wet walk around what is now called Little Lake (an offshoot of the Otonabee River in Peterborough), they found accommodations at MacFarlane's Hotel. From there, they were able to contact Sam, who paddled a canoe ten miles down the Otonabee rapids to welcome them. Besides Sam, they had introductions to two Peterborough-area families, the Ephraim Sanfords and the Thomas A. Stewarts, both of whom did much to help them during their early months there.

For about a week the Traills stayed with the Sanfords (he was a local merchant and the postmaster). They then proceeded north to Sam's log house, which he had named Reydon Cottage after his Suffolk birthplace. Here they looked over their land on the lake, and

Another genteel settler, Anne Langton, sketched the Otonabee at Peterborough (above) in 1837.
"How wild!" she wrote. "A waste wilderness of wood … to say nothing of the stumps."
Her 1852 watercolour of the river (below) shows how the scene had changed in fifteen years.

Sam helped Thomas to examine land adjacent to his military grant and to make arrangements to build a house on a favourable site on his property. That home, however, would not be completed for several months because of delays in arranging for building supplies and finding skilled workmen. In the meantime the Traills moved around among family and friends, settling in happily for several weeks in late September at Auburn, the large home of Thomas and Frances Stewart on the east bank of the Otonabee River about two miles north of Peterborough. An Anglo-Irish family with eight children, the Stewarts were neighbours and business partners of Robert Reid, having emigrated to Upper Canada with the Reids in the winter of 1822–23.

During their stay, Frances Stewart became both a mentor to and a close friend of Catharine. Frances and Catharine shared literary and botanical interests as well as English social assumptions and a strong religious

Broken China in the Snow

On a morning in early February of 1834 the Moodies loaded all their possessions into two wagons fitted out with runners for the trip to Douro. After a long, jolting journey around the edge of the Cavan swamp, they were still travelling after nightfall when a large, fallen pine tree blocked their path. The first sleigh cleared it successfully but the second "hung poised upon the top of the log, was overturned with a loud crash…. Alas, for my crockery!" Susanna wrote, adding "I knew that no fresh supply could be obtained in this part of the world." Unlike Frances Stewart's china (right), which had arrived intact from Ireland, Susanna's Coalport tea service, a wedding gift from her mother, was gone forever.

faith.[6] Frances, who had struggled with her own uncertainties as a settler, had much to teach her younger friend about how to live and make do uncomplainingly in an environment where goods were in short supply and social contacts were limited. She knew that patience, perseverance and fortitude were much-needed qualities in a pioneering woman, especially one who had been "delicately nurtured."

Catharine proved an apt and eager pupil, always willing to help with the domestic duties and to gather practical information of various kinds. Through Frances, she "learned more practical lessons for my guidance in the new life of a settler's wife in the backwoods than any book could have given me, had any book been written on the subject." Catharine's cheerfulness and her reverent attention to Frances helped her, in turn, become a mentor to several of Frances's daughters, especially the delicate thirteen-year-old Ellen, who was inclined to melancholy and fits of rebelliousness.

The Traills moved to Sam's homestead in late November to oversee completion of their house. Thanks to Frances, it was a well-prepared Catharine Traill who took over her own home on December 8, 1832, after what she described as "many untoward and unavoidable delays." She and Thomas named their first Canadian home Lake Cottage, for it was built with a view of Lake Katchewanook and of Sam's property to the south. It is likely that Catharine returned to stay with the Stewarts during the latter stages of her first pregnancy and the birth of James George, in June 1833. Auburn provided a comfortable refuge and was closer to Peterborough and the medical attentions of Dr. John Hutchison.[7]

On January 7, 1834, Catharine wrote to James and Emma Bird in Suffolk, in part to assure them that their son James, who had come over with the Moodies, was thriving as a worker on Sam's farm. She also proudly described the comforts and amenities of their new bush home: there was a nice parlour with a glass door opening towards the lake, and a Franklin stove to provide heat for the Canadian winter; a bedroom, pantry and kitchen, also on the main floor; a cellar below; and an upper floor that could be divided into three bedrooms. They had plaited Indian rugs, a handsome sofa that doubled as a bed, green cambric blinds on the windows lightened by white muslin draperies, painted chairs, a bookcase and some large prints and maps.[8]

Thirteen months later, the Moodies moved north from Hamilton Township to take up their land grant to the north of the Traills. Only a mile-long walk through the woods above the lakeshore now separated the sisters. When Susanna arrived, she found an experienced and happy Catharine, proud of her new home, prouder still of her eight-month-old son — its "greatest ornament" — and well served by her capable nurse and helper, an older Irish woman named Isabella Gordon.

These were generally very good times in the bush, especially for Catharine. And overall, the future looked promising. Immigration continued unabated despite the threat of cholera, and property values looked solid. A government survey of the upper reaches of the Otonabee River, the area's lifeline and transportation route, suggested that the waterway would soon be improved. Catharine was delighted with their new log house in the bush and enraptured by her young son, and Thomas Traill was still optimistic about their future, even if he continued to keep his own counsel about his debts and long-term financial worries. By means of paid Irish loggers called "shanty-men" and a logging bee, he had managed to clear and fence about twenty-five acres by November 1833 and had produced a crop of oats, corn, pumpkins, potatoes and turnips in his first year. In addition, a legacy of £700 that Catharine, like her sisters, received from an uncle in England allowed Thomas to buy additional acreage adjacent to his property and pay off a part of his nagging debts.

Things would perhaps never be better for the Traills than they were during those early years. The small social world of Peterborough — "a very genteel society, chiefly composed of officers and their families, besides the professional men and storekeepers" — and of fledgling Herriot's Falls (Lakefield) had welcomed them and, for Catharine at least, the experience had measured up to many of her expectations.[9] When Susanna arrived with her family by sled in February 1834, she found herself buoyed by Catharine's good will and affection. She and John would enjoy their own "halcyon days" in Douro that spring and summer, little aware of the tests and disappointments that lay ahead.

Genteel Settlers

From Frances Stewart, Catharine would learn "how much could be done ... to make a home in the lonely woods the abode of peace and comfort." The Stewarts had emigrated from Ireland ten years earlier and had carved a homestead from raw wilderness. Their large log home now boasted a piano and was decorated with collections of dried flowers, Indian pottery and rock samples, and the Stewart children joined Catharine enthusiastically in gathering even more specimens. Catharine later recalled "the bright blazing fire in the parlour of Auburn, enlivened by the conversation of its genial, intellectual host and hostess," and considered her time with the Stewarts "some of my happiest days beneath the pine of Douro."

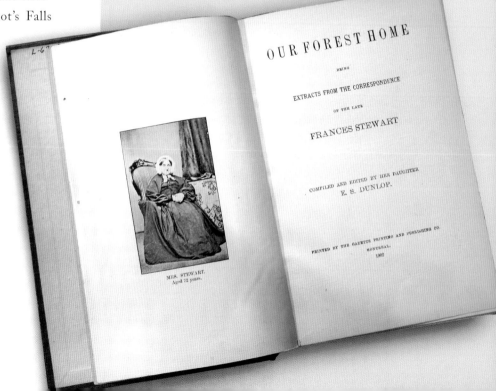

OUR FOREST HOME

BEING

EXTRACTS FROM THE CORRESPONDENCE

OF THE LATE

FRANCES STEWART

COMPILED AND EDITED BY HER DAUGHTER
E. S. DUNLOP.

PRINTED BY THE GAZETTE PRINTING AND PUBLISHING CO.
MONTREAL
1902

MRS. STEWART.
Aged 72 years.

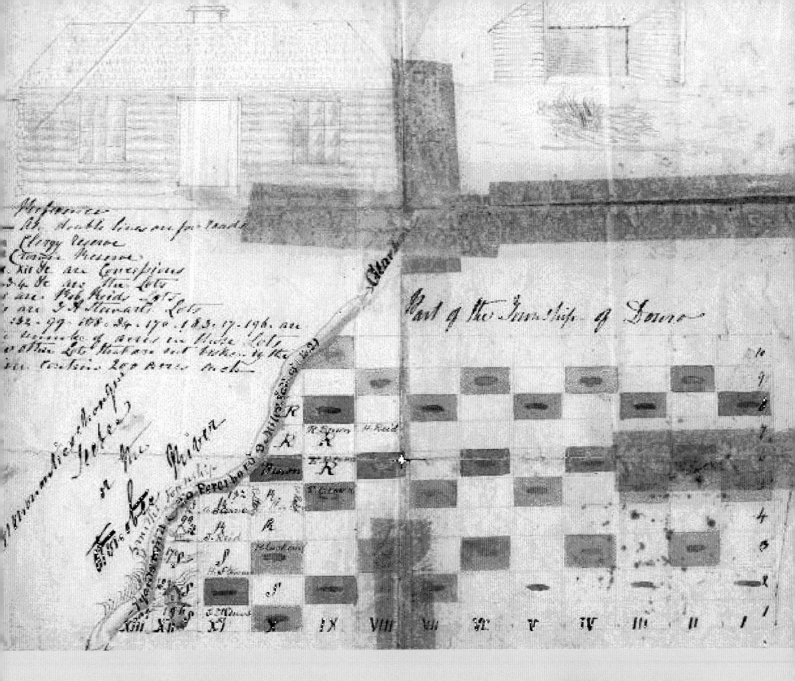

Frances Stewart drew this map of settlement in Douro for a cousin in Ireland. The grey and pink rectangles signify Clergy and Crown reserves, and lots belonging to the Stewarts and Reids are labelled "S" and "R." The log house she sketched is similar to one preserved today at Lang Pioneer Village (right) near Lakefield. A silhouette (opposite, top) is believed to be of the young Frances Stewart. A photograph of her in old age appears on the title page of *Our Forest Home,* a collection of her letters published posthumously in 1889 (opposite).

CHAPTER SIX

Sisters in the Backwoods

THE SPRING AND SUMMER OF 1834 WERE HAPPY times for both Catharine and Susanna. They were together once again and each had a new log home to organize and a new child to dote upon. Sam and his family were nearby, and there were a few female neighbours who lived close enough to provide agreeable companionship on occasion. Their husbands had farming challenges to engage them, and they could take hope in the optimistic views shared by the leading figures in the vicinity of Herriot's Falls.

At first, discouraged by the loss of her home in Hamilton Township and by the grey, wet conditions of a prolonged February thaw, Susanna looked at her backwoods surroundings "with jaundiced eyes." She felt alienated by "the cheerless waste," which she found "murky" and "reeking." Many of the white pines of the Douro forest rose over 120 feet in height, so that even within a cottage clearing one felt enclosed by towering trees.

A watercolour by Philip Bainbrigge of a bush farm near Chatham shows the tall trees, rail fencing and corduroy road so familiar to the sisters. Bainbrigge was a British officer who served in Canada from 1838 to 1842.

The Moodies stayed with the Traills for the first week while the interior of their one-storey log house was partitioned into rooms. Catharine became Susanna's bush mentor, outfitting her with moccasins for freer movement in the underbrush, helping her to quell her "foolish dread" of wild beasts and encouraging her to focus upon the interesting natural details of their forest environment. "My conversation with her," Susanna reported, "had quite altered the aspect of the country, and predisposed me to view things in the most favourable light." Susanna made the transition to the backwoods more quickly than she had expected, mostly because of her sister's cheerful influence.

In fact, the Moodies' first spring in Douro was "spent in comparative ease and idleness." Susanna carefully organized her cedar-log house into "a nice parlour, a kitchen, and two small bed-rooms," establishing comfortable living quarters for John, herself and their two daughters as well as their servants, John Monaghan and a young woman named Mary. But before any planting could be done, some of their land had to be cleared by shantymen, even though the cost was formidable.

Since their cows remained for a time in Hamilton Township awaiting herding north, there were fewer chores and they spent their leisure hours wandering the lakeshore and paddling in a light cedar canoe that John had purchased. They fished on the lake and explored the shoreline and small islands, relishing "the pure beauty of the Canadian water." Feeling like "first

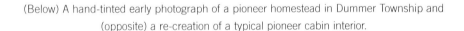

(Below) A hand-tinted early photograph of a pioneer homestead in Dummer Township and (opposite) a re-creation of a typical pioneer cabin interior.

discoverers," they found themselves "charmed with the freedom and solitude around us." Unlike Catharine, Susanna became, in her own words, "quite a proficient in the gentle craft" of canoeing — a backwoods skill not expected of a genteel woman.

Both Catharine and Susanna were fascinated by the comings and goings of several Native families who had long considered the Lake Katchewanook area one of their traditional hunting grounds. Several families of the Chippewa, or Mississauga, tribal affiliation camped on the Smith Township side of the lake at certain times during the year. When fish and game were plentiful, the women crossed the lake to trade with the white settlers along the Douro shore. Sam Strickland had begun bartering with these families in 1831, and within a few years the Traills and the Moodies were also participating in these exchanges, which were usually initiated by the natives. They gave their white

(Right) This 1867 painting by John H. Caddy is believed to be a depiction of the Moodies' farm on Lake Katchewanook, though it was painted twenty-eight years after their departure. The structure at extreme right may be the original cabin. (Below) The lake from near the cabin site today.

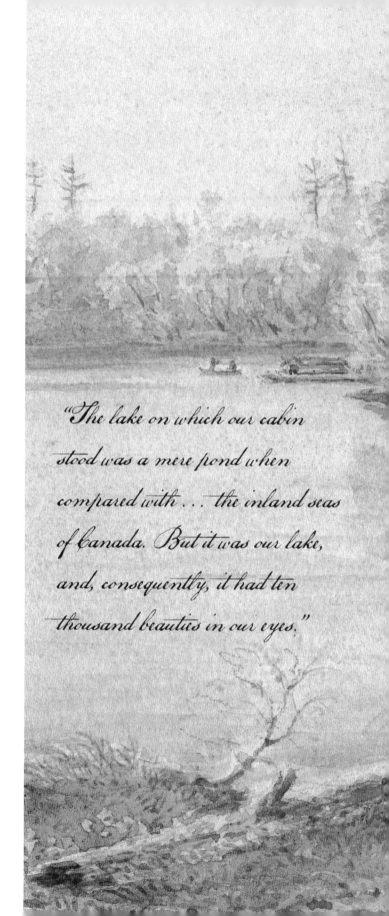

"The lake on which our cabin stood was a mere pond when compared with . . . the inland seas of Canada. But it was our lake, and, consequently, it had ten thousand beauties in our eyes."

"Our Indian Friends"

1847- Squaws of the Chippeway Tribe.

"A family of Indians have pitched their tents very near us." begins Catharine's description of Native people in *The Backwoods of Canada*. This encampment may have resembled one sketched (above) in 1837 by travel writer Anna Jameson (a London acquaintance of sister Agnes) during her Canadian sojourn. The Chippewa women (depicted, at left, by J.O. Lewis) soon came to barter with Catharine, who found them "of gentle and amiable dispositions … and very honest." She admired their crafts, and a small birchbark canoe (below) was sent to her sister Sarah at Reydon. Susanna, by contrast, found that their "beauty, talents, and good qualities have been somewhat overrated," though she did admire the Indians' honesty and kindness and found that they were never "familiar, coarse or vulgar" — a claim she could not make about many of her other neighbours.

neighbours colourful nicknames — Sam was *Chippewa* (the bald-headed eagle) and Susanna *Nonocosisqui* (a hummingbird, which she deemed "a ridiculous name for a tall woman") — and on occasion they invited the settlers to visit their wigwams. The settler families welcomed these exchanges and were pleased to hear the Natives sing Christian hymns that they had learned from Methodist ministers near Rice Lake.

In many ways, these encounters helped to define the backwoods experience, and it was perhaps inevitable that Catharine and Susanna would write about them. They also knew that Native life in North America was a subject of considerable interest to British readers and that their observations would be carefully scrutinized for authenticity of detail. Naturally, the women, whom they saw more often during bartering visits, won their special attention. Schooled in phrenology by Robert Childs, Catharine, and particularly Susanna, took a close interest in reading their facial features to probe more deeply into lives that were strange but fascinating to them. They also had good reason to be grateful for the help and support that these women provided in times of need.

Catharine's *The Backwoods of Canada* was mostly written in 1834, after only a year and a half of actual living in the bush. She had kept detailed journals of her experiences and botanical observations. Drawing upon those notes, which included drafts of some of her letters home, she created a text written as "Letters from the Wife of an Emigrant Officer." Agnes Strickland showed the manuscript to several publishers early in 1835. She found her man in Charles Knight, the publisher for the Society for the Diffusion of Useful Knowledge, a benevolent foundation that published material for the education of the lower classes. Having an immediate need for a new text to include in a series called "The Library of Entertaining Knowledge," Knight pounced on the opportunity he saw in Catharine's manuscript. *The Backwoods of Canada* appeared in London in two parts in January 1836 and went through numerous printings in its first decade. Its usefulness to potential emigrants was enhanced by the pleasures of its narrative and the agreeable way in which the author presented herself. However, it would be more than a year before Catharine received her own copies and could present Susanna with a signed edition.

Susanna had too much to contend with on the home front at this time to write anything substantial, though she continued to send poems to newspapers like the Cobourg *Star* and the New York *Albion*. In 1835–36 she was invited to send whatever material she had on hand to Sumner Lincoln Fairfield, the editor of the *North American Quarterly Magazine*. But however much Fairfield admired her poetry and was eager to publish her work, he could offer her no remuneration; she even had to bear the cost of postage to send her work to him in Philadelphia. She must have envied Catharine her well-earned success with *The Backwoods of Canada* and the £110 she was paid, an amount that Thomas Traill was very glad to receive, given his debts.

But nothing in Catharine's book foreshadowed how bad life would become in the next year. With the success of *The Backwoods* in London, she prepared a sequel, drawing on sketches and observations written in and after 1835, but that manuscript never became a book. For a fuller look at life in the backwoods of Upper Canada during the last half of the 1830s, readers must turn to *Roughing It in the Bush* and Catharine's later sketches, and surviving letters.

Why the darkening change in conditions? The reasons are several and interconnected. As settlers, the Traills and Moodies had to cope with the inescapable and persistent ague, a malarial fever transmitted by mosquitoes that often incapacitated a pioneer for weeks at a time. In addition, a major economic depression affecting Europe and the United States during these years had a devastating effect. Prices for wheat and farm goods plummeted, and the government of the colony had to withdraw promised funding for the development of roads and canals. One result of the prolonged stagnation was the unrest that led to the rebellions in the Canadas in 1837–38.

While the Traills and the Moodies proceeded to develop their farms and test out possibilities for investments, they soon realized that there was a noticeable falling-off of new immigrants[1] and that money was becoming increasingly tight. The seriousness of this downturn became clear at a time when both Thomas and John had disposed of their wives' recent inheritances and money was again scarce for both families. Concerned about his ability to develop the property in which his equity was located, Thomas Traill put his farm up for sale and grew increasingly depressed about the prospects before him. As always, John Moodie was watchful for other opportunities but, having sold his military pension for steamboat shares, he had no steady income to fall back on. (And since the *Cobourg* did not prove to be a good investment, he was forced to finally sell his shares at a loss.) Moreover, he soon became aware that the quality of his land in Douro was far below that of his Hamilton Township farm and that in coming north they had likely given up their best chance to get ahead.

Meanwhile, Catharine and Susanna were busy coping with the demands of childbirth and motherhood. Between 1834 and 1838, as conditions steadily worsened in the bush, each of them had three children. By the fall of 1838, Catharine had four young children in total and Susanna five. It is difficult to imagine today just what the demands of pregnancy and childbirth were like in the backwoods at this time. Servants were hard to find and seldom stayed for long. Professional medical aid was twelve miles away along what were, at best, rough roads. To dwell in any detail on these matters was not a part of the genteel prescription practised by writing women of the period. In "Our Logging-Bee," however, Susanna describes conditions at the time of the birth of Dunbar, her first son, which occurred during a sweltering heat wave in August 1834. "I was very ill," she recalled, "yet for hours at a time I had no friendly voice to cheer me, to proffer me a drink of cold water, or to attend to the poor babe." John was battling the ague and trying to spend as much time as he could manage in the fields, while lit-

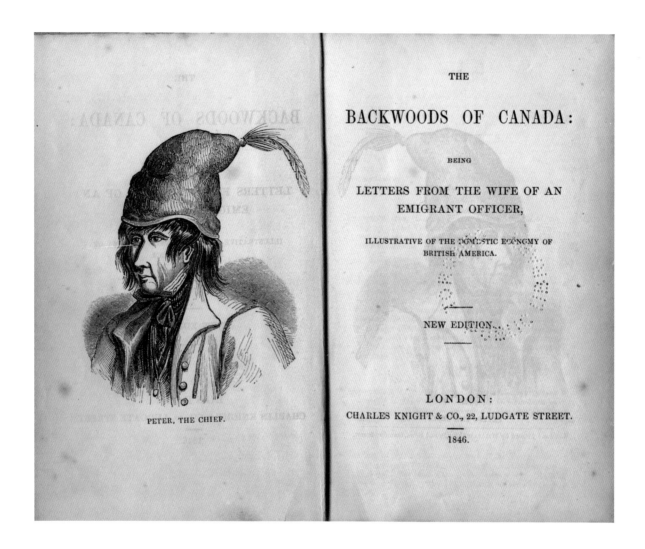

PETER, THE CHIEF.

THE

BACKWOODS OF CANADA:

BEING

LETTERS FROM THE WIFE OF AN EMIGRANT OFFICER,

ILLUSTRATIVE OF THE DOMESTIC ECONOMY OF BRITISH AMERICA.

NEW EDITION.

LONDON:
CHARLES KNIGHT & CO., 22, LUDGATE STREET.
1846.

Catharine's *The Backwoods of Canada* received glowing reviews and became required reading for those contemplating emigration to North America. Her optimistic view of life in the New World, however, had yet to be tested by the real hardships she would later encounter. Although it was a steady seller for the publishing house of Charles Knight, its author received a flat fee for the copyright to the book and no royalties on copies sold.

By 1900 the Moodie cabin on Lake Katchewanook had disappeared, but the hand-dug well was still visible.

took shape in a manuscript that presented a different view of pioneering than the positive one offered by Catharine. While, for instance, Catharine praised the efficacy of bees as communal efforts that provided much-needed help to settlers, Susanna presented them in *Roughing It* as dangerous, lawless and wasteful events that typically cost the host far more in losses than he gained in work accomplished. In her account of the three logging bees undertaken for them during the stifling summer of 1834, she notes the carelessness of bush workers in regard to the danger of fire and the proper care of animals, and conveys her outrage at the excesses of a Captain Lloyd who got drunk and encouraged others to do the same. Lloyd had a reputation for neglecting his wife and children and beating his servants while under the influence. Susanna could not forgive such behaviour, especially in a person of her own class. Her chapter "The Walk to Dummer" describes a wintry mission of mercy that she undertook with two friends to help Lloyd's struggling wife Louisa and her children, who had been abandoned in the Dummer bush.

Volume Two of *Roughing It in the Bush* provides a compelling record of the ways in which pioneer women helped one another. They would visit to provide comfort or needed supplies, offer homespun medical support

tle Aggie, who was also suffering from the illness, lay pale and comatose beside her, "so cold and still, with half-closed violet eye, as if death had already chilled her young heart in his iron grasp." With all those around her suffering from the ague and with no servant available, Susanna managed to see to her family's needs, despite her own weakness. "Often did I weep myself to sleep," she recalled, "and wake to weep again with renewed anguish."

But backwoods mothers could afford little time for self-pity. Among the many things that Susanna learned in the bush was how to draw on her physical strength in ways she had never before thought possible. She would need this during the next five years of hardscrabble living. Memories of these years later during illnesses and pregnancies or take a child into their home as a way of providing relief for a struggling mother. In this regard, Susanna's record is significantly quiet on the extent of the help that Catharine offered her in times of need. In these omissions the reader may sense a temporary cooling of their relationship. Certainly, Thomas Traill appears more frequently in Susanna's recollections than does her sister. While this may simply have been a function of his greater mobility outside the house, there is some evidence that a certain distance developed between the sisters. One contributor to this may have been Charlotte Emilia Shairp, a recently married young woman who lived in a pleasant log cabin just north of the Moodies. Emilia was the daughter of an army major who had retired to a villa called Endsleigh Cottage, near Peterborough. She had married her cousin, Alexander Mordaunt Shairp of the Royal Navy, and they had settled on a lakeside grant in north Douro. But her husband, like Lloyd, was something of a drinker, and it was not long before he abandoned farming for a return to naval service. When Emilia was not back in Peterborough with her parents, she was at her bush home, and she often visited other genteel women in the vicinity. Catharine likely met her first, and in *The Backwoods* she describes a pleasant visit to Emilia's home by canoe in September of 1834. However, the presence of Susanna, whose home was situated between Catharine's and Emilia's, seems to have changed the dynamic of that friendship. Susanna's close relationship with Emilia became a constant during her bush years and she appears with some frequency in *Roughing It*. During this same period, there are fewer

references to Catharine than one might expect, and mere domestic busyness does not explain her absence, as she lived only a half-hour's walk away.

The latter half of *Roughing It in the Bush* is about elemental struggles far removed from comfortable drawing rooms. Susanna describes several occasions when fire threatened their very lives. There was a near-conflagration when their log house was being completed, a brush fire that resulted from an ill-timed attempt by a young helper to burn the fallow surrounding their cabin, and a roof fire caused by overheated stove pipes during the winter (a very frequent danger for pioneering families). She recalls terrifyingly wild summer storms that tore wide swaths through the bush and threatened everything in their path. She describes her canoeing adventures, such as being caught on the lake by sudden wind and storm. And she makes clear what it was like to undertake demanding labour on the farm when there was no money to hire help, stating with pride, "I have contemplated a well-hoed ridge of potatoes on that bush farm, with as much delight as in years long past I had experienced in examining a fine painting in some well-appointed drawing-room." She lauds poverty as a school in which she has learned much about herself, even as she struggles to maintain the standards that her background and education had given her. It is little wonder that her book still speaks movingly to many readers, for it is about self-awareness and a closer relationship to the natural world. It is also about learning to adjust conditioned expectations to meet real and pressing needs. For Susanna, the backwoods become a template for self-discovery.

CHAPTER SEVEN

Rebellion and After

To the surprise of many, armed rebellion broke out in Upper Canada on December 4, 1837. William Lyon Mackenzie, an outspoken newspaper publisher and former mayor of Toronto, led a ragtag group of armed rebels down Yonge Street to Montgomery's Tavern. After a brief skirmish and only few casualties, government troops were able to disperse the rebels. Fuelled by anger over the advantages enjoyed by special interests within the colony, the uprising challenged the authority of the British colonial government and, in particular, the leadership of Lieutenant-Governor Sir Francis Bond Head. "Galloping" Head's many abuses of power and refusal to listen to the concerns of the citizenry had fanned discontent into open strife. In the remote backwoods of Douro, however, the Traills, Moodies and Stricklands saw the situation unambiguously: Mackenzie was a traitor acting in defiance of British rule; the rebels were a misdirected and unruly lot who had dared to call the time-honoured traditions of English governance into question and deserved swift judgement.

Rumours about the rebellion abounded: large numbers of rebels, including Natives, had attacked and burned Toronto; Americans had crossed the border in support of the rebels; chaos was about to break loose! Answering a proclamation circulated hastily throughout the province on December 5, 1837, Sam Strickland and Thomas Traill left immediately for Peterborough to join a militia unit being mustered there to advance to Toronto. John Moodie received the news too late to join his brothers-in-law and, in any case, was not thought to be fit to travel as he was nursing a broken bone in his leg. Not one to be left behind, John set out on his own for Peterborough a day later, only to arrive well after the militia unit had departed for Port Hope. Borrowing a horse from Emilia Shairp's father, he made his own way to Toronto with another group of volunteers. There he learned the truth behind the

Lieutenant-Governor Sir Francis Bond Head's hostility to Reformers and meddling in an
election helped bring on the rebellion of 1837, led by fiery newspaper editor William Lyon Mackenzie (opposite).
Bond Head (above) was recalled early in 1838 and never held office again.

VICTORIA *the* 1st *and* REFORM.

BIDWELL *and the* GLORIOUS MANORITY

1837 *and* A GOOD BEGINNING.

In early December of 1837 a band of roughly 400 rebels marched south on Yonge Street in Toronto. Armed with rifles, staves and pitchforks, as depicted in this drawing by C.W. Jefferys, the men clashed with a group of militia soldiers and volunteers led by Colonel James Fitzgibbon, a hero of the War of 1812. The skirmish took place just south of Montgomery's Tavern, near present-day Eglinton Avenue, and Mackenzie's followers were quickly dispersed. Afterwards, a nine-foot banner created by the rebels (above, front and back) was captured at Montgomery's Tavern and remained in the possession of the Bond Head family for many years. It reveals how the ascension of Queen Victoria in 1837 was a spur to the winds of reform in Upper Canada.

rumours: the battle on Yonge Street had been minor, the insurrection had been put down and the villainous Mackenzie had fled towards the United States via the Niagara District. But unease was still very high in Toronto and across the province. There were rumours of other planned acts of rebellion and renewed fear of organized invasion from the United States. Memories of the War of 1812 and the burning of Toronto were still vivid in the minds of many.

Drawing on his experience in the Napoleonic Wars and his local connections, John was able to gain a captaincy in a newly-formed Toronto military unit, the Queen's Own Regiment. His official instructions were abrupt and specific: return home immediately, set your house in order, purchase a uniform and return to Toronto by mid-December to train a company. The excitement of his appointment was a welcome tonic. Suddenly, he could see a break in the economic gloom and an end to his apparently futile labours in the backwoods. He would have a salary for at least six months, as well as a position of respect and authority, and he could contribute to his new country in a way for which he was well qualified.

When John hurriedly returned to the bush farm to carry out his preparations, he realized that he had been wise to proceed on his own to Toronto. The Northumberland militia unit, which included Sam and Thomas, had gone no farther than Port Hope before learning that their services were not required in Toronto. They returned to their farms but were called on to participate in training exercises in Peterborough and to patrol the back townships in pursuit of skulking rebels. Thomas would injure himself

in a fall from his horse during one exercise and lose his militia position. Dogged by bad luck, as he saw it, he sank further into depression. Sam, on the other hand, settled rather happily into the military to-do of a captaincy — his first such position and one that burnished his local prestige.

While the rebellion gave John Moodie renewal as a soldier, it inspired Susanna to pen several patriotic poems. The first of these she sent off to Toronto with John, who quickly placed it with a friend, Charles Fothergill, who was about to publish the first issue of his newspaper, *The Palladium of British America*. An elderly Englishman with extensive journalistic experience in the colony, Fothergill warmed to Susanna's patriotic defence of British institutions and proudly included her "Canadians, Will You Join the Band: A Loyal Song," in the first issue of the *Palladium* on December 20, 1837. In an editorial comment he glowingly hailed Susanna as a "Daughter of Genius — and Wife of the Brave."[1]

In fairly rapid succession, Fothergill printed a number of Susanna's poems,[2] many of which found favour with other newspaper editors in the Canadas. Her "Canadians, Will You Join the Band" was reprinted at least nine times within a month. But the best possible response came from distant Montreal, where John Lovell, then operating a newspaper called the *Montreal Transcript*, reprinted her poem in his December 28, 1837, issue. Lovell saw in her a potential contributor to *The Literary Garland*, a new magazine he was preparing to launch, and that spring he wrote to her with promises of prompt payment at acceptable rates for both poetry and prose.

Susanna reprinted her patriotic poem about the rebellion (below) in *Roughing It in the Bush,* although she described it as an "outpouring of national enthusiasm which I found it impossible to restrain." Given that the Moodies' sympathies soon swung to the side of the Reformers, lines like "'God and Victoria!' be your cry/And crush the traitors to the dust" might have made even Susanna blush. The poem, however, brought her to the attention of Montreal publisher, John Lovell (left), whose new magazine *The Literary Garland* would become an important showcase for her work.

AN ADDRESS TO THE FREEMEN OF CANADA

Canadians! Will you join the band –
    The factious band – who dare oppose
The regal power of that bless'd land
    From whence your boasted freedom flows?
Brave children of a noble race,
    Guard well the altar and the hearth;
And never by your deeds disgrace
    The British sires who gave you birth.

What though your bones may never lie
    Beneath dear Albion's hallow'd sod,
Spurn the base wretch who dare defy,
    In arms, his country and his God!
Whose callous bosom cannot feel
    That he who acts a traitor's part,

Remorselessly uplifts the steel
    To plunge it in a parent's heart.

Canadians! will you see the flag,
    Beneath whose folds your fathers bled,
Supplanted by the vilest rag
    That ever host to rapine led?
Thou emblem of a tyrant's sway,
    Thy triple hues are dyed in gore;
Like his, thy power has pass'd away –
    Like his, thy short-lived triumph's o'er.

Ay! let the trampled despot's fate
    Forewarn the rash, misguided band
To sue for mercy, ere too late,
    Nor scatter ruin o'er the land.

The baffled traitor, doomed to bear
    A people's hate, his colleagues' scorn,
Defeated by his own despair,
    Will curse the hour that he was born!

By all the blood for Britain shed
    On many a glorious battle-field,
To the free winds her standard spread,
    Nor to these base insurgents yield.
With loyal bosoms beating high,
    In your good cause securely trust;
"God and Victoria!" be your cry,
    And crush the traitors to the dust.

In *Roughing It in the Bush*, Susanna speaks of hearing from Lovell as a sudden and wonderful occurrence, even though it followed directly from the patriotic poems she had sent to Fothergill. Still, it led to a paying outlet for her writing that she had long hoped for. By May 1839, she was a contributor to the pages of *The Literary Garland* when Lovell published another of her patriotic poems, "The Oath of the Canadian Volunteers: A Loyal Song," along with her tribute to the river that flowed south from her Lake Katchewanook home, "The Otonabee."

The reverberations of Susanna's poems were also felt in government quarters. After the incompetent and heedless Sir Francis Bond Head was relieved of his duties in February, the newly appointed lieutenant-governor, Sir George Arthur, arrived in Upper Canada to oversee the defence of the province. He, too, was charmed by Mrs. Moodie's patriotic poetry, and when she wrote him in the summer of 1838 to ask for his help in improving her family's situation, Arthur was well disposed to take a personal interest. Early that autumn he announced a second six-month appointment for John, this time as paymaster for the militia units protecting the northern shore of Lake Ontario.

Despite the success of her patriotic poems, Susanna's life on the Douro farm was neither easy nor without anxiety through 1838 and much of 1839. With

Sir George Arthur

John away and some income assured from his military service, she ran the farm efficiently, paid a portion of their debts and kept the household in order, with only the servant Jenny Buchanan to help her. Susanna won the praise of Thomas Traill, who wrote to Moodie in May 1838:

Your wife … has commended the esteem of every one. Your spring crops are nearly in … In fact she is farther advanced than her brother or me, or indeed any of the neighbours … all your children look fat, fair and flourishing … and you will find on your return which I hope will be soon that every thing has been managed admirably in your absence.

It was a tribute that must have heartened John Moodie, who had been assigned to patrol the Niagara District along the north shore of Lake Erie, a task which, for the most part, he found static and dispiriting. His monthly letters home to Susanna reveal the tedium of his duties, but also his great affection for "my old woman and our dear brats." "I could not live long without seeing you all," he told her. Sending money back to her when possible, he begged for her patience and continued strength, never doubting her resourcefulness under pressure. As spring gave way to summer there was little evidence of any threat from across the border, so he was released from service and he returned to the farm in July of 1838.

Together again, the Moodies enjoyed a fine late summer and autumn. "The harvest was the happiest we ever spent in the bush. We had enough of the common necessaries," Susanna wrote in *Roughing It*. John was present for the birth of their third son, John Strickland, in September and shared with Susanna a special delight in this beautiful child. When he set out in late November to meet his commanding officer, Baron George de Rottenburg, in Belleville, he departed in sadness but with renewed confidence in his wife's capabilities and ingenuity.

For Susanna, however, the winter of 1838–39 would prove to be a traumatic time. Alone again, with only Jenny Buchanan for adult company, she showed her usual durability, sufficiently regaining strength from her pregnancy to organize daily activities, prepare manuscripts for Fothergill and Lovell and keep up her correspondence. In a thank-you letter to Sir George Arthur on December 18, 1838, she advocated for the needs of the Traills and requested a military appointment for the kindly and neglected Thomas. After a Christmas celebration at Catharine's cabin, she became aware of a painful breast infection (mastitis) that had developed while she was breastfeeding baby John. Within days she was in great pain and, as she vividly described to John, lay "like a crushed snake on my back unable to move or even to be raised forward without the most piteous cries." After ten days of agony, Thomas Traill walked the twelve miles down to Peterborough on a cold December night to urge Dr. John Hutchison to attend his sister-in-law. Hutchison came up immediately and lanced the abscess that had developed in her infected breast.

The doctor's quick action may well have saved Susanna's life. Describing the amount of fluid that drained from the cut and continued for days after, Susanna wrote that "I was often quite out of my senses, and only recovered to weep over the possibility that I might never see my beloved husband again." The sturdy Jenny Buchanan proved an adequate nurse as the illness continued, but Hutchison was appalled at the condition of the dark and dirty cabin. In a way that Susanna could never forget, he blurted out, "In the name of God! Mrs. Moodie, get out of this."

But there was no getting out for the time being. There were kindly offers of help and opportunities to sell or lease the land, but John was cautious, fearful that his paymaster's position would last only six months and that to move his family to Belleville might prove disastrously expensive. Susanna was uncomfortable in accepting offers of charity. Even though Emilia Shairp had hurried to Douro to nurse her through her recovery, Susanna rejected a proposal that she and the children join Emilia and Louisa Lloyd in Peterborough. In her weakened state, she continued to breastfeed John and do her best to keep work on the farm in some sort of order.

The mastitis was only the beginning. While Susanna was still bedridden, young Donald took a

The Country Doctor

A native of Kircaldy, Scotland, John Hutchison practised medicine in Peterborough from 1830 until his death from typhus in 1847. A stone house built for him in 1836 by the residents of the town survives today as a museum and displays his medical kit, which includes tools to cut through bone as well as the alcohol used as a disinfectant. His account ledgers record visits to the homes of both "Lieutenant Traill" and "Captain Moodie," and his birth registers mark the deliveries of five of the Traill children. To the Traills he was also a close family friend, and Catharine's story, "The Old Doctor," is clearly a portrait of John Hutchison. She draws on phrenology when describing the shape of his head as indicating "mental power, firmness and decision" and believed his "keen blue fiery eye" and "mouth slightly sarcastic" conveyed his decisive character. It is not difficult to imagine such a man stating bluntly in his Scots burr that Susanna should quit her backwoods life as soon as possible.

(Opposite) An illustration by Lynne Clifford-Ward of Dr. Hutchison tending a sick baby was based on a period portrait (above) of him as a young man.

running fall into the edge of the stove and cut his head open to the bone. Sam and Thomas helped to deal with the cut but could not prevent a large scar from forming on the boy's forehead. By mid-January Susanna felt "tamed down" by her illness and far less resilient than before John's departure for Belleville. The fierce storms of February made the family suffer dreadfully from the cold, as she did not dare to overheat the stovepipes. Then, in March, two of her children were hit by a severe influenza that, she learned, had taken the lives of numerous youngsters in the Peterborough area. First, Donald fell ill, and then little John became comatose and convulsive. Susanna "expected every hour that they might breathe their last." In this instance Dr. Hutchison, who was overwhelmed with the epidemic in Peterborough, refused to come north. However, another Peterborough doctor did come to her aid, helping both children to recover and providing a regimen for Susanna who had also been affected by the virus. Catharine offered immediate help and, again, Emilia Shairp came up to provide support for Susanna.

While John wrestled with keeping strict account of the money he was distributing to the troops from Belleville, Susanna carried on, buoyed by his monthly letters. "Your tenderness reconciles me to every thing," she told him. Her sense of loneliness was compounded in early March when the Traills completed the sale of their farm to George Wolseley, a retired Anglican minister from England.[3] By mid-March, Catharine and Thomas had relocated to a small rented house near Peterborough. It was close to the Stewarts, and the reunion and close contact with Frances Stewart was a welcome tonic for Catharine. On March 20, Susanna wrote to John:

> *The dear Traills are gone — I am doubly lonely now. Many tears have I shed since their removal, we have been on such happy terms all winter. They have been so kind to me especially poor Traill. One knows not the value of a friend till one is left alone in this weary world. The poor children quite fret after their good aunt.*

Such comments suggest that "happy terms" may not always have been the case between the sisters and that the kindly Thomas had provided Susanna with more sympathy than her sister. Still, her sense of loss at Catharine's departure was great. "I begin to get tired of the woods, and now that the dear Traills and Mrs. Shairp are gone, I care not how soon we follow." An escape from the bush would not, however, improve Catharine's own weakened state in her new home. She remained ill and semi-bedridden for months after a difficult pregnancy and delivery, and had to struggle with newborn Annie's precarious health throughout that time.

That winter, the news from home told Catharine and Susanna that their sisters Agnes and Eliza had been busy on the publishing front. Following upon Eliza's articles on royalty for Henry Colburn's *Court Journal*, they had hit upon the idea of a series of books under the general title "Memoirs of the Queens of England from the Norman Conquest." Colburn had quickly agreed to publish them, and with the industrious Eliza taking the lead in research, they had produced two volumes by 1837. They even managed to obtain permission to dedicate the books to the new queen, Victoria, who had ascended to the throne in June of that year. Although Eliza would write eight of the thirteen "memoirs," by sisterly agreement, only Agnes's name appeared on the title page.

For Susanna and Catharine, the saga of "The Queens" must have seemed like a fantasy. The reviews of the first two volumes had been very strong, and Agnes had achieved a new level of popular recognition that they, in the remoteness of the colonial bush, could only dream about. Catharine's sequel to *The Backwoods of Canada* had died a quick death among London publishers, and Susanna's sole current hope was *The Literary Garland*, the first issue of which she deemed "a wretched performance." Meanwhile, they marvelled at Agnes's appearances at major events involving the young queen, including a special court ceremony in 1838 where Agnes was one of several women presented to Victoria.

The spring of 1839 provided little relief for Susanna's loneliness and weariness. On March 20, she wrote to John that the last three months "… have been months of sickness anxiety and sorrow, and worse than all, of absence from you. There are times when I almost wish I could love you less. This weary longing after you makes my life pass away like a dream. My whole mind is so occupied with thinking about you that I forget every thing else." On April 4, the day of their eighth wedding anniversary, she slyly reminded him of their

Some of the volumes in the "Queens of England" series.

shared ardour: "I dreamt you returned last night, and I was so glad, but you pushed me away, and said that you had taken a vow of celibacy and meant to live alone, and I burst into such fits of laughing that I awoke."

Still, it was a capable, if dispirited, pioneer who kept to the tasks at hand — she continued to manage the farm, to pay off their debts as best she could, to endure excruciating toothaches and to see that the children were cared for at home or well watched over by others. An attempt in late March by the Peterborough sheriff to seize their cattle disturbed her tremendously, both for the embarrassment and how it reflected upon her fine sense of social respectability. She allowed a young friend to care for Agnes for several months and sent young Dunny to her neighbour, Hannah Caddy, for a time when illness was affecting the other children.

In her letters she provided John with descriptions of the antics of the children and the routine of the farm, but she continued to lament their long separations:

> *A state of widowhood does not suit my ardent affections. Anxiety destroys my health. I have not suffered so much sickness since I have been in Canada as this winter.… Every year convinces me of the madness of gentlemen attempting to farm in the bush, wasting their education, mind, manners, and property in drudging as pioneers. It quite reverses the general order of things.*

An expert now in "drudging," she could only hope for an escape from the bush and a renewed contact with society once John returned and they could think through their situation together. As the spring dragged on and John's return was delayed several times by his continuing duties, she grew more despondent and frustrated. His position had been formally terminated, but he had much to do in auditing and completing his records as paymaster. His superior, Baron de Rottenburg, spoke confidently of exerting his influence on his behalf; John knew that he had a good friend in the baron and wanted to complete his work as reliably as possible.

Meanwhile, Susanna waited, an impatient but enduring Penelope. She painted images of birds and flowers on tree funguses to be sold in Peterborough and wrote poems and stories for Lovell. Her letters of June 1 and July 5, 1839, cry out with a mixture of strength and gratitude on the one hand and anxiety and disappointment on the other. Her health, she realized, was now far better than Catharine's and, following a recent visit by Thomas, she was concerned both about her sister's condition and brother-in-law's despondency. Susanna's letter of June 1 shows her reviving strength and continuing resolve, but by July 16 she was fraught with frustration at John's continuing absence, which had now extended to six weeks:

> Your long absence and silence, paralises all exertion.... I know not what to do about the farm, and I am so dispirited that I care nothing about it. I have no money to hire labor to cut the grain and the crop is but indifferent.... Oh heaven keep me from being left in these miserable circumstances another year. Such another winter as the last will pile the turf over my head.

Little did she know that John's letter of July 5, which crossed with hers in the long lag of delivery time, carried the best possible news for their future prospects. Sir George Arthur's secretary had written to John, no doubt at Baron de Rottenburg's urging, to promise that an "office" would be offered to him at "the first possible opportunity." Arthur also wanted John to understand that he made this promise "not only on your own account, but from the esteem and respect he entertains for Mrs. Moodie."

The final months of 1839 were charged with excitement. John's return revived Susanna and the children. Beyond the joy of their long-postponed reunion, there was the news, gazetted widely in the Canadas, that John had been appointed the sheriff of the newly-formed Hastings County. The family would move to Belleville as soon as John could arrange accommodations for them.

John went back to Belleville in the early fall, bent upon arranging his "sureties" and making arrangements for both his new office and his family. On November 24 he wrote to Susanna, agreeing that they should lease the Douro farm and sending her additional money to help prepare for the move. At the same time he was, by then, well aware that his appointment had stirred up a hornet's nest of controversy and anger, especially among Tory supporters and office-seekers in the Belleville and Kingston area. Though he had served as paymaster for close to eight months in Belleville, he was seen as an outsider and, even worse, a Reform sympathizer, a puppet of Sir George Arthur. Over the past two years, John had become aware that the Conservative forces in Upper Canada had much to answer for with regard to inequities in the province. While maintaining his loyalty to England, he was now a supporter of the Durham Report and an advocate for effective political change. He told Susanna that he was acutely sensitive to the severity of partisan feelings in Belleville and pledged to steer a middle course as best he could. The fact that the professional core of Belleville society was strongly conservative in its leanings concerned him greatly, "but by steadily pursuing a conciliatory course to all I trust by the blessing of God we may be the means of doing much good."

As 1839 drew to a close, Sam Strickland took the Moodie family and Jenny Buchanan in his lumbering sleigh from the backwoods to Belleville to begin their new life. The trip took three days. With characteristic regret, Susanna lamented leaving "that humble home consecrated by the memory of a thousand sorrows."[4] She worried that she had aged considerably during her five years in the bush and that she would no longer be able to adapt to a life with increased social activity. She had had a final visit from Emilia Shairp and sold off all but the furniture and accessories of the farm to Reverend Wolseley, the new owner of the Traill farm, who also gave her good spiritual counsel in her anxious state. Sadly, as they advanced south to Belleville via Peterborough, there was no opportunity to visit the Traills. And so, a long sleigh ride ended what Susanna would later call "this great epoch of our lives."

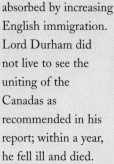

The Durham Report

A noted reform-minded politician, John George Lambton, 1st Earl of Durham, was sent from Britain in 1838 to investigate the causes of the rebellions in Upper and Lower Canada. He stayed only five months, and his Report on the Affairs of British North America was published in February of the following year. It recommended a modified form of responsible government, the creation of a supreme court and a uniting of Upper and Lower Canada and the Maritime provinces. He believed that the cause of the rebellion in Lower Canada was ethnic conflict and wrote that Canada consisted of "two nations warring within the bosom of a single state." In Upper Canada he thought that power was monopolized by "a petty, corrupt, insolent Tory clique," and advocated that the majority party in the Assembly should take more responsibility for governing. For Lower Canada he recommended that French-Canadian culture be absorbed by increasing English immigration. Lord Durham did not live to see the uniting of the Canadas as recommended in his report; within a year, he fell ill and died.

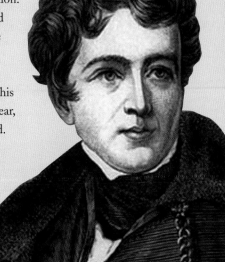

CHAPTER EIGHT

"A Change in Our Prospects"

THE TRAILLS AND THE MOODIES WERE NOT LONG in realizing that an escape from the backwoods was no antidote for concerns about health and children or continuing fears for the future in a new country. For the Traills, the decade of the 1840s would prove to be a difficult and gloomy struggle in which the spectres of poverty, illness and bad decisions dogged them relentlessly. By contrast, life improved dramatically for the Moodies once John took up his position as sheriff of Hastings County. There were many adjustments to be made in moving to Belleville, but they at least had a source of income, a house with numerous amenities and the promise of an improved social life.

John soon realized, however, that the anger over his appointment as sheriff would not quickly dissipate. He reported to Susanna that one hopeful for the sheriff's job, a former magistrate, Tory and Orangeman named Thomas Parker, was "half crazy" with disappointment and "like to bite the ends of his fingers off." And Parker was not alone in wishing Moodie ill. In Belleville, resistance to the very idea of "responsible government" as outlined in the Durham Report was a consuming passion for its conservative elite. The Kingston *Whig* led the attack on both Sir George

Arthur and Moodie early in the autumn of 1839, labelling John "an out and out advocate of *Responsible Gov't.*" And indeed, John had shifted his political sympathies to the hopeful outlook espoused by Robert Baldwin and the Reformers he led in the provincial assembly. Though he was well aware of the charged atmosphere he was entering, John's plan was to be as neutral as he could, especially in political and electoral matters. He joked with Susanna that it was his strategy to attend both the Anglican (Tory) and Presbyterian (Reform) churches and to seek medical advice from both of the leading doctors (the one Tory, the other Reform.)

John's position required that he serve a huge geographical jurisdiction, stretching northward from Lake Ontario beyond such distant villages as Bancroft and Marmora. His job was to keep the peace for the entire county, oversee local elections and process legal actions. What made him particularly vulnerable, however, was the

This view of Belleville (opposite) by English artist George Ackermann dates from 1870. The headquarters for Sherriff Moodie (right) were in the county jail, located in the back of the stone Hastings County Courthouse that crowns the slope at left.

"A CHANGE *in* OUR PROSPECTS"

101

Three scenes of Belleville in 1830 by Thomas Burrowes show the Moira River (top) above the town, (middle) at Bridge Street, just down the hill from the Moodie cottage, and (bottom) as it flows into the Bay of Quinte.

fact that his income was based on his ability to serve notices and collect fines rather than a salary. First off, a Conservative judge named Benjamin Dougall made it difficult for John to obtain approval for his "sureties," or guarantees, as sheriff by rejecting the men he had nominated as guarantors and requiring him to find others.[1] Once John was formally on the job, the Tory lawyers of Belleville set out to hinder his efforts to claim money that should have been available to him. John was resentful of the fact that the Tories insisted on claiming all the loyalty to England for themselves, labelling any other views as radical and republican.

In more placid Peterborough, the Traills were experiencing trials of a different kind. After leaving the backwoods in March 1839, they had settled for a time in a cottage on the Stewarts' property in South Douro. Over the next few years they moved at least twice, first to a small, rented house in Ashburnham, "the Scotch village" across the river from Peterborough, and then to a farm in Otonabee Township, which they called Saville after one of Thomas's childhood homes in the Orkneys. During these years Catharine continued to write when she was able, but her energies were too often sapped by her own illnesses, the needs of her growing family and persistent worries about money.

She had pinned high hopes on her sequel to *The Backwoods of Canada*, but Agnes could not find a publisher for it and, according to Catharine, in 1842 it "still remain[ed] a dead letter" in her sister's hands. Agnes had already resorted to breaking up the manuscript in order to place some of its sketches (letters) with publishers she knew. These appeared in such British magazines as *Chambers's Edinburgh Journal* and

Agnes and the Queen

Agnes managed to secure a pass to Queen Victoria's coronation on June 28, 1839, and her family at Reydon received a breathless, detailed description. So did her publisher, Henry Colburn, who was quick to see the commercial potential of an Agnes-penned book on both the Queen's coronation and her forthcoming wedding. Hurried into print after the royal nuptials in February of 1840, *Victoria from Her Birth to Her Bridal* portrays the young queen as a model of piety, kindness and marital devotion. Despite this, the book did not please the subject herself. After receiving a copy, Queen Victoria (right) pencilled notes such as "not true" "entirely false" and even "absurd" on many of its pages. A lady-in-waiting neatly copied these comments in ink (below) and forwarded them to Agnes (left) with a letter expressing the Queen's desire that corrections be made. A deeply mortified Agnes appealed to Henry Colburn, but he refused to consider amendments, knowing the book would sell well regardless, and it did.

QUEEN VICTORIA.

110   the sanction of her royal highness the Duchess o Kent. Nevertheless it was necessary for the queen to speak as queen; for such of our readers as are little versed in courtly etiquettes may not be aware that, whether regarding the selection of a partner for life or a partner for a dance, it devolves upon a queen regnant to declare her choice and select her own. And the following is perhaps the more authentic statement of the manner of the royal intention :—

"Her majesty inquired of his royal highness whether his visit to this country had been agreeable to him?—whether he liked England?—and on the answer being given "exceedingly." "Then," added the queen, "it depends on you to make it your

Sharpe's London Magazine, but provided precious little income to the struggling Traills. In March 1842, Catharine wrote directly to Lord Henry Brougham, the patron of the Society for the Diffusion of Useful Knowledge in London, asking for more money on the basis of the continuing sales of *The Backwoods of Canada*. The result was a further payment of £15, which capped her earnings from the book at £125.

Agnes, meanwhile, was marching onward to become *the* royalist historian in the eyes of many of her countrymen. Catharine and Susanna could only envy Agnes's letters, in which she reported on her visits to aristocratic estates, and marvel at an elder sister who could claim friendships with figures whose names were household words among the well-informed in Britain. Her 1840 quickie book on the young monarch, *Victoria from Her Birth to Her Bridal*, had added to that reputation, even though the Queen herself was highly critical of much of its biographical detail.

Catharine's uncertain health was a matter of continuing concern throughout these years. Good friends like the Stewarts rallied around her, providing considerable support, particularly during her illnesses and difficult pregnancies. From 1840 through 1843, Catharine lost two of three children either during childbirth or from an illness in early infancy. During these years, her husband's debilitating depressions increased, seemingly triggered by the difficult conditions facing his family. An eccentric, sweet-tempered and acutely sensitive individual, Thomas had long suffered from bouts of depression, and the more his Canadian family sank into poverty, the greater was his awareness of his own incapacity. By 1840 it was clear

that Westove, the family estate in the Orkneys to which he was legal heir, would never provide him with an income. His two sons who had stayed behind in Edinburgh were completing their educations, but refusing to fulfill one of Thomas's cherished hopes by joining Catharine and his new family in Canada. What income he had could only forestall bothersome debts for a time, and the money he earned through real-estate transactions, like the sale of his Douro property, provided only temporary relief.

Thomas and Catharine applied for help to Lieutenant-Governor Sir George Arthur and his successor, Lord Sydenham, but none was forthcoming. While Thomas willingly served as a local magistrate and nurtured his numerous friendships among the Peterborough gentry, he watched helplessly as his family's situation worsened month by month. For a time, Catharine's manuscripts raised hopes of fresh income, as did the plan she hatched in 1839 to start a small school in their Ashburnham home. Thomas's unmarried Scottish sister-in-law, Barbara Fotheringhame, was invited to come out to help her in its operation. When she did not come, Catharine tried her hand at teaching, only to have to close down the school when a maternity-related illness left her too weak to continue.

Boxes sent from Reydon continued to help them meet their needs, but each year the Traills' situation grew more distressful. Worries about small debts, schooling for her children, their lack of clothes and the struggle to put food on the table weighed heavily on Catharine. Annie Traill remembered how her mother soon trained her daughters, particularly Kate, to help with a range of domestic duties. Despite the gloom projected by Thomas's moods, Catharine made the Traill household as happy a place as she could manage. In later years her children recalled those darkening days with fondness, remembering the cheerful expeditions she organized and her storytelling on winter nights.

As the decade progressed, the Traills edged closer to bankruptcy, and by 1846 matters had reached a desperate state. By then, Willie (born in 1844) was a cheerful presence, but there were six children to feed on virtually no income.[2] Relief came from an admirer of Catharine's, the Reverend George Bridges, who offered them his Rice Lake home rent-free for a year while he returned to England. His residence was an unusual one: a garrison-like tower near the lakeshore to the west of the village of Gore's Landing. Dubbed Wolf Tower by Catharine, it was a six-storey octagonal building, consisting of one room per floor, with several outbuildings joined by tunnels.

Bridges was an eccentric Englishman who had settled in Jamaica before a tragic accident claimed his four daughters. In his distraught condition, he had chanced to read Catharine's *The Backwoods of Canada*. Greatly admiring both the book and the positive outlook of its author, he decided to move to Canada. He sought Catharine out while visiting Peterborough, where he occasionally took services at St. John's Church, and they became friends. Wolf Tower presented its own challenges, both in terms of heating and daily domesticity, but the time the family spent there was a welcome hiatus during a bleak period.

In Belleville, the Moodies, too, were facing challenges. The leading spokesman of the Conservative party, publisher George Benjamin,*(continued on p 109)*

The Strange Gentleman

George W. Bridges was one of the most exotic characters ever to fetch up in the Canadian backwoods. A tall, elegant man with a fondness for silk robes and, it was said, for opium, Bridges had been the rector of a parish church in Jamaica with an island-born wife and six children. One day in 1834, his wife boarded a ship for England without notice; Bridges followed her, but she refused to see him or the children. Then his parents and eldest son, too, chose to ostracize him. Bridges returned to Jamaica and within a year saw his four daughters drown in the sinking of a pleasure barge. Claiming that if he had not "gone wild he would doubtless have gone mad," Bridges fled to Canada with his youngest son. In 1838, Catharine wrote of "the strange gentleman" who was building a "fanciful prospect residence" near Gore's Landing to "divert his mind from the heavy pressure of family affliction." After the Canadian climate drove Bridges back to England, he allowed the Traills to occupy the octagonal tower he had built on the shores of Rice Lake.

Wolf Tower

"It was a most beautiful situation and … a very remarkable building," remembered Annie Traill of Wolf Tower. "We had never seen one at all like it and it was so delightful to be near the lovely lake." The design of the tower may have been influenced by phrenology, one of whose noted practitioners claimed that octagonal houses bestowed contentment. And Wolf Tower did give a measure of that to Catharine. "I came in weak health," she wrote, "but so renovating did I find the free, healthy air of the beautiful hills that in a very short time I was able to ramble about with my children among the picturesque glens and wild ravines of this romantic spot." The tower itself was built of wood and covered with blue-grey plaster. The entrance was through a heavy, oak door in the hillside (dubbed Traitor's Gate by Catharine), which opened on an underground passage that led to the kitchen. Cedar-lined dining and drawing rooms occupied the next two floors, then came bedrooms and a storage room. The windowed belvedere that was used as a schoolroom crowned the top. "On looking back," Annie Traill continued, "I do not think [it] could have been a convenient house to live in, so many stairs must have been tiring for Mother who was not very strong … but we young ones … thought it PERFECT and were happy as larks."

Cedar Swamp. Rice Lake.

An 1850 watercolour of Rice Lake shows Wolf Tower in the centre. An impression of the view from the tower can be seen in an 1854 painting (opposite, top), done from the church in Gore's Landing. (Opposite) An artist's conception of Wolf Tower, which burned to the ground in 1856.

kly Intelligencer.

RE BE HARMONY IN THINGS ESSENTIAL—LIBERALITY IN THINGS NOT ESSENTIAL—CHARITY IN ALL.

LLE, ONTARIO, COUNTY OF HASTINGS, THURSDAY, MA 9 1889.

THE "Y" DISASTER VICTIMS

COMPLETE LIST OF THE KILLED IN THE RECENT ACCIDENT.

The Remains of Seven Still Recognized as Identification is F

HAMILTON, May 4.—...

AMONG THE DEAD.

for Missing Friends Among the ed Bodies at Hamilton.

May 3.—The best preserved of bodies have been identified, or as have the most clothing at...

TRADE AND TRAFFIC.

Leading Features of the Grain and Produce Markets at Home and Abroad.

TORONTO, May 7.—St. Lawrence market was quiet yesterday. Little was offered and there was slack demand. Quotations: Butter, pound rolls, 23c. to 25c.; large rolls, 19c. to 20c.; inferior, 15c. to 17c. Lard, tubs, 12c. to 13c. Cheese, 12c. to 13c. Bacon, 10c. to 11c. Eggs, fresh laid, 12c. to 13c. Chickens, 70c. to 90c. per pair. Geese, 8c. to 9c. per lb. Turkeys, 12c. per lb. Ducks, 80c. to $1. Beets per bag, $75 to...

PARNELL TAKES IT BACK

HE THINKS NOW THAT HE WAS MIS-TAKEN ON FRIDAY.

His House of Commons speech Referred to Ribbonism and Was Fairly Accurate—General Cable News.

LONDON, May 7.—The Parnell Commission resumed its sittings today. Mr. Parnell upon taking the stand said he desired to correct that part of his evidence given Friday in rela tion to the statement made by him in the House of Commons concerning the non-exist ence of secret societies in Ireland. Upon re ferring to the Hansard reports of the proceed ings of the House he found that his remarks which had been quoted by Attorney-General Webster referred particularly to ribbonism at...

ALL FOR TEN CENTS

Reason of the Border Troubles ternational Railway Car

WASHINGTON, May 7.—The qu exacting a duty upon every p built car that enters the Unite does not appear to be giving the Department a great deal of con though it is under consideration being regarded by some of the western people who are interested with a good deal of anxiety. Th troversy is an old one renewed. Th vival of interest has been attribu leged growing indifference of the rail people to be governed by the internati understanding that only cars used in transportation of the international free should be exempt from the impost duty.

used his newspaper, the Belleville *Intelligencer*, to scrutinize the sheriff's actions and to mock his attempts to run a middle course between Tory and Reform factions. Benjamin, a former Montrealer, hid his Jewish roots and played a leading role among the area's strong contingent of Orangemen. Whenever possible — or so it seemed to Susanna — the *Intelligencer* took a perverse joy in wronging her husband.

One of John's duties as sheriff was to serve as the electoral officer for Belleville and area, and the first election for the United Province of Canada was called for April of 1841. It did not help John's difficult situation that Robert Baldwin, the newly appointed solicitor general of Canada and the leader of the Reform party, was asked by the lieutenant-governor, Lord Sydenham, to run for a seat both in Toronto and Belleville. Baldwin's presence on the Belleville ballot angered the local Tories. The incumbent was Edmund Murney, a well-connected and socially prominent lawyer who, ironically, was Baldwin's cousin by marriage. Despite the familial link, there was no love lost between the two opponents.

Although Moodie was personally but quietly a committed Baldwin supporter, he knew that it was his duty to oversee the election in an objective and orderly fashion. This meant keeping the peace at two local polls while voting took place over several days. It did not help that reports were circulating that he and Susanna had entertained Baldwin during one of his campaign visits to town. In Belleville, no such action went unnoticed.

During the election, the usually restrained Murney surprised Moodie with his platform antics, labelling Baldwin a rebel and a papist and challenging his opponent's integrity without ever addressing the actual issues. He particularly appealed to members of the Orange Order, some of whom crowded the hustings, waved weapons and threatened reprisals against those voters they taunted as "radicals." John Moodie did his best to keep order as voters approached the poll, where they were required to proclaim their choice in front of a heckling crowd of observers.

Baldwin won the 1841 election by the narrow margin of thirty-five votes; however, Thomas Parker, a disgruntled Tory and former rival for John's job, was quick to launch both a formal appeal of the results and a call for a review of the behaviour of the returning officer. Neither appeal was upheld, but a post-election dispute between the new lieutenant-governor, Sir Charles Bagot, and elected members of

In addition to being the editor of the Belleville *Intelligencer*, George Benjamin was a grand master of the Orange Order and became Canada's first Jewish MP in 1856.

Robert Baldwin

The Moodies first met the man who would become known as "the father of Responsible Government" shortly after their arrival in Belleville. Robert Baldwin impressed them with his gentlemanly integrity and vision of how Canada should be governed. Susanna was charmed by the fact that he not only admired her work but was a poet himself. His air of romantic melancholy also appealed to her — Baldwin still grieved intensely for his wife who had died in 1836. The Moodies' friendship with Baldwin brought John's impartiality into question during the elections of 1841 and '42, and melées at the polling stations led to John's removal as returning officer.

the Legislative Assembly led by Baldwin resulted in another provincial election the following year.

From John Moodie's point of view, nothing could have been worse. By now, partisan feelings in Belleville were running so high that violence could likely not be avoided. Worried particularly by the threats and actions of the local Orangemen, John eventually called in government troops and closed the polls early, a decision for which he was maligned in the press.[3] With Murney leading at the time, John's action was interpreted as a manoeuvre to aid Baldwin. Even though Murney himself had signed a paper at the polling station agreeing that there had been serious voting irregularities, he would subsequently turn on the sheriff. A Tory-initiated petition was more successful on this second occasion, with the result that John was relieved of his duties as returning officer and Murney was awarded the election. Baldwin wisely conceded the victory to Murney, secure in his Toronto seat and another in Rimouski in Canada East.

A chastened John Moodie may have been grateful to be relieved of his electoral responsibilities, but he felt no such relief in his daily work as sheriff. Nuisance suits and strategies to undercut his earnings continued in the Belleville courts, while the *Intelligencer* took delight in criticizing his conduct. All this exasperated Susanna and, as usual, her outlet was her pen. In 1843, a story entitled "Richard Redpath, the Voluntary Slave" appeared as a short serial in *The Literary Garland* as well as in a new Toronto newspaper called *The Star*. Set in Jamaica, its subject was "the abhorred trade" in slaves in the West Indies, but a prominent figure in the story was the editor of

110

The Jamaica Observer, one Benjamin Levi, who loudly supported slavery and deemed its opponents "traitors to Great Britain and enemies of their country." The parallel between Benjamin Levi and George Benjamin was readily evident to Belleville readers. Mixing her skills as a caricaturist with an overcharged anti-Semitism, Susanna undertook to expose the covert "Jew Editor" of the Belleville *Intelligencer*. She offered her readers "a true picture drawn from life, which so closely resembles the original, that it will be recognized by all who ever knew him, or fell under his lash. A man *detested* in his day and generation."

This calculated act of revenge was fully justified in her mind by Benjamin's actions, but it revealed that, however liberal she might have become in such matters as opposing slavery, she readily dispensed anti-Semitic aspersions, fully confident that her audience would find them acceptable. The villain and the Jew blend together in "Richard Redpath" as in much contemporary Victorian fiction, and the fact that she later included the story in her collection *Matrimonial Speculations* (1854) suggests that she had no regrets about her attack.

Although Belleville's social structure, ticklish politics and size (there were 1,500 residents in 1840) took some getting used to, the community did offer educational opportunities for her children, a range of domestic comforts, new social acquaintances and more time for her writing. Between 1840 and 1849, Susanna became *The Literary Garland*'s most productive writer, providing a serialized novel or memoir — along with numerous stories and poems — nearly every year. The writer in her revelled in the opportunity to be paid for her work and to be publicly recognized. It took several years, but her name — Mrs. Moodie — became one to reckon with in the colony by 1846.

Having lived through two frightening fires that threatened their log home in the Douro bush, it seems almost ironic that the Moodies were "burnt out" in December 1840 in Belleville. This calamity came at a time when their resources were still thin and the town's firefighting capacities were laughably inadequate. The promptness of neighbours helped to save many of their belongings, however, and they experienced numerous instances of kindness from friends and neighbours in the fire's aftermath.

Yet nothing could soften the anguish that Susanna endured in the deaths of two of her children in the early 1840s. George Arthur Moodie, fondly named for the lieutenant-governor who had helped them escape the backwoods, died one month after his birth in July 1840. But it was the death of five-year-old Johnnie that shook Susanna to the core and cast a long shadow over her memories. He was her last child born in the bush, she had nursed him lovingly through her frightening bout of mastitis in late December 1839, and she had been frantic when, as a two-year-old, he went missing for about half an hour during the 1840 fire.[4]

Johnnie's death was an accident of the sort that all parents fear. While fishing with his two older brothers in the Moira River, he decided to run home to show his mother the fish he had caught. But in his haste to get away he slipped on a wet dock, fell into the turbulent river and drowned. The date was June 18, 1844. It was "the saddest and darkest [hour] of my sad

JOHN STRICKLAND,
DROWNED
IN THE BAY OF QUINTE,
JUNE 18, 1844,
ÆE. 5 Y'rs 8 Mo's.

GEORGE ARTHUR,
DIED AUG. 8, 1840,
ÆE. 1 MONTH.

CHILDREN OF
J.W.D. & S.S. MOODIE

The Early Lost

"The shade of death upon my threshold lay,
    The sun from thy life's dial had departed;
A cloud came down upon thy early day,
    And left thy hapless mother broken-hearted –
           My boy – my boy!"

"Long weary months have pass'd since that sad day,
    But naught beguiles my bosom of its sorrow;
Since the cold waters took thee for their prey,
    No smiling hope looks forward to the morrow –
           My boy – my boy!"

"The voice of mirth is silenced in my heart,
    Thou were so dearly loved – so fondly cherish'd;
I cannot yet believe that we must part,–
    That all, save thine immortal soul, has perish'd –
           My boy – my boy!"

My lovely, laughing, rosy, dimpled, child,
    I call upon thee, when the sun shines the clearest;
In the dark lonely night, in accents wild,
    I breathe they treasured name, my best and dearest –
           My boy – my boy!"

"The hand of God has press'd me very sore
    Oh, could I clasp thee once more as of yore,
And kiss thy glowing cheeks' soft velvet bloom,
    I would resign thee to the Almighty Giver
Without one tear – would yield thee up for ever,
    And people with bright forms thy silent tomb,
But hope has faded from my heart – and joy
Lie buried in thy grave, my darling boy!"

– Susanna Moodie

eventful life," she later wrote in *Life in the Clearings*, where she included her heartfelt poem "To the Early Lost," which declared that "the voice of mirth is silenced in my heart."

Between the deaths of George Arthur and Johnnie, the Moodies were heartened by the birth of their fourth and last son, Robert Baldwin Moodie, in 1843. Though they kept Robert's middle name as quiet as possible when dealing with the testy Conservatives in Belleville, the naming represented a proud gesture of familial support for their friend and his vision of responsible government for the Canadas.[5]

The latter half of the 1840s were better years for the Moodies, despite the painful loss of their much-loved son. Susanna kept up her writing for *The Literary Garland*, while John's work as sheriff became more routine and increasingly remunerative, in part because the Tory leaders were, if not more sympathetic to the grieving parents, at least less hostile to him on a daily basis. In an 1845 letter to Baldwin, John reported that "even our enemies felt our great loss." But at the same time he realized that he would be better off if he kept an even lower political profile in the future.[6]

Two experiments marked these quieter middle years of the decade. In August 1844, perhaps seeking consolation after Johnnie's death a few months earlier, the Moodies were among the twelve founding members of a Congregational church in Belleville. Their involvement recalled Susanna's excited conversion to Congregationalism in 1830 and reflected their disappointment with both the Anglican and Presbyterian churches in town. However, their connection with the group was short-lived. Within less than a year, the Moodies were expelled, or "excommunicated," for what the church defined in its minute book as "disorderly walk." This was an allusion, presumably, to the Moodies' laxness in performing churchly responsibilities and perhaps their refusal to confine their social connections to the narrow life available within the congregation.

The second experiment was the launching of *The Victoria Magazine* for publisher Joseph Wilson in September 1847. As editors, John and Susanna sought out likely subscribers and gathered material from other writers, wrote new pieces and revised old works, reviewed books and observed cultural activities of interest. They tried to create an inexpensive periodical that would help to improve the tastes and literary interests of the populace of the Canadas. In its twelve issues one finds pieces by Strickland family members — Sam from Douro (identified as "Pioneer"), the now-famous Agnes in England and Catharine. It was here that Susanna presented her autobiographical serial "Rachel Wilde: or, Trifles from the Burthen of a Life" in nine chapters as well as the first two chapters of what would become *Roughing It in the Bush*.

What the pages of *The Victoria Magazine* particularly reveal is the shift in Susanna's writerly focus from traditional narrative forms to the autobiographical. Separated now by three decades from her girlhood days in Suffolk and by seven years from her bush experiences, and with two of her children in the Belleville cemetery, she answered an inward compulsion to revisit her formative experiences. In releasing herself from the stifling bonds of story, she gained a freedom that enlivened and empowered her writing. Susanna Moodie, whether called Rachel Wilde or, still later, Flora Lyndsay, emerges as her own major subject in a way that was unusual among women writers of the time. *Roughing It in the Bush*, *Life in the Clearings* and the fictionalized *Flora Lyndsay* would allow her to complete the process of self-realization and self-justification in which she was deeply engaged.

For Catharine, however, writing had proved a difficult task during the early 1840s. Despite the opportunities made available to her through Susanna's widening literary connections — there was the opportunity to contribute to *The Literary Garland* and to provide stories for *The Victoria Magazine* — Catharine's output was small, a function of her still-unsteady health (a weak back and rheumatism) and the increasing demands of her family on her time. The Traills lived in Wolf Tower for a year, then, for two years, they rented a farm near the village of Gore's Landing which she named Mount Ararat. In the restorative atmosphere of the Rice Lake Plains her health steadily improved, so much so that she encouraged Thomas to set about finding a permanent home for the family in the area. They settled upon a log home and farm above the south shore of the lake. Thomas arranged to sell his half-pay pension and, with the help of the Moodies, Sam Strickland and a wealthy Peterborough friend, was able to arrange a mortgage on the farm. Thus, in 1849, after ten years of uncomfortable moves and painful retrenchments, the Traills could once again claim ownership of their own property. The farm, which they called Oaklands, offered

*sufficient for them, and hoping to meet each other
the right hand of the Judgement seat of Christ.*

*Belleville Canada W.
August 19. 1844.*

*John Woods.
Jn. H. Meickell
John Fry
W. Dunbar Moodie
Susanna Moodie
Atira Merill
Rufus Holden
Josephine C Fry
Elizabeth Holden
Mary. Meickell
Hannah X Cole
mark*

Withdrawn.

Expelled
Expelled.

The small Congregational church that the Moodies helped found in 1844 was one of the earliest of its kind in Canada. This denomination favoured simple houses of worship (left), and each congregation was responsible for determining its own religious principles. Those for the Belleville church are strongly stated in a preamble recorded in its "minute book," which was signed by the Moodies (above) and ten others in August, 1844. Just as strongly worded were the minutes for April 2, 1845, which stated that the church would withdraw from the Moodies "as from those who walk disorderly" and declared them "excommunicated from church fellowship and privileges." The congregation would disband two years later.

"It was a lovely evening that I first descended Mount Ararat ...
The Islands lay almost at our feet, some in deep shade, and others
just catching the last radiant glance of the retiring sunbeams.
A deep indigo tint was on the distant shore, and all looked so
lovely, that I could have lingered there as long as a ray of twilight
remained to lighten the landscape." Catharine Parr Traill in *Forest and Other Gleanings*

splendid views of the lake and its many islands. It was located about two miles from Gore's Landing where, to Catharine's delight, an Anglican Church named St. George's was already under construction.

Catharine gave birth to her final child, Walter, in 1848 while they were still at Mount Ararat. But once she was firmly settled in the Rice Lake area, she was able to resume her old writing habits, realizing that stories for publication represented one possible form of income that might supplement what Oaklands could produce for her family. Her creative energies re-emerged strongly in the 1850s, inspired in large part by her new surroundings and the way she and her children flourished in that landscape. Rice Lake and its environs would fire her imagination at least as much as her Lake Katchewanook home in the backwoods.

CHAPTER NINE

The Decade of the Book

AS THE 1850S BEGAN, THE TWO STRICKLAND SISTERS in Canada emerged from their personal struggles to become well-known figures in the literary life of the developing colony. The decade was a more settled time for both their families, and therefore conducive to the daily work of writing or copying manuscripts and preparing them for publication. By its end, the two sisters had published nine books — three from Catharine and six from Susanna, beginning with Susanna's personal epic of pioneering, *Roughing It in the Bush*, in 1852.

By 1850 the Traills were well established at Oaklands, their farm near the village of Gore's Landing. Though living far below what we now call the poverty line, the family carried on as productively as possible, dependent on

the farm work of the older boys, amused by the high spirits of the younger children and inspired by the renewed vigour of Catharine. The eldest daughters, Kate and Anne, eased the pressures of Catharine's life considerably by ably addressing the family's daily needs in clever and economical ways. The oldest sons, James and Hal, on the other hand, likely chafed at their subservience to the plough and their father's eccentricities and all-too-frequent bouts of excessive emotionality or

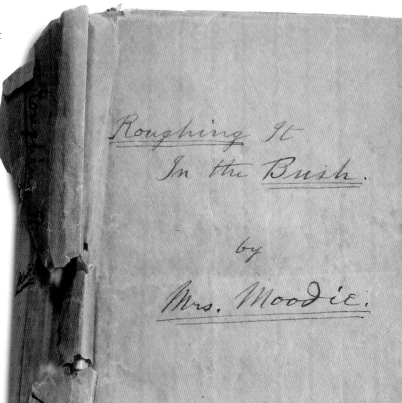

The hardships Susanna had endured and written about in her bestselling book *Roughing It in the Bush*, are clearly visible on her face in this photograph from the early 1850s.

depression. Despite their mother's pleas, they were sometimes unable to prevent themselves from voicing their increasing dissatisfaction with their father.

In Belleville the Moodies had slowly carved out a private life that involved social connections with some of the town's families of note, mostly those of the Reform persuasion. While John's work as sheriff was never free of legal challenges or acts of nuisance from his Tory opponents, he had come to know his job well and undertook his responsibilities carefully. The older Moodie boys were moving towards careers and marriages, while the girls, Katie and Agnes, found congenial suitors through connections in Belleville.

For Catharine, two writing projects loomed large. One was a series of sketches and stories that she entitled *Forest Gleanings*. She wrote these descriptive pieces, several of which are charming and vivid evocations of the Gore's Landing landscape, for *The Anglo-American Magazine* (1852–56), a new Toronto periodical that, for a time, replaced Montreal's *Literary Garland* as the leading literary journal of the day. The other was a novel for adolescents, set near the Rice Lake Plains and based on her fear of losing a child in the backwoods. From her early days in Douro, Catharine had been concerned about the dangers of children becoming lost in the woods. Such stories

transfixed early settlers and were passed among them at bees and during social visits; no mother was immune from such a worry when, within a matter of minutes, a playful child could become lost in the maze of forest and bush that surrounded most log homes. When the daughter of Cobourg-area businessman Thomas Eyre disappeared from a picnic in 1837 and was lost for four days, the story grabbed front-page attention in the Cobourg *Star*. In her Douro log cabin with three small charges of her own, Catharine clipped and saved the article, realizing its potential both as a compelling narrative and a cautionary tale.

Catharine sent her novel for young readers to England in the late summer of 1850. For nearly two years, Agnes Strickland held on to the manuscript while she sought out a publisher and edited the text with help from Jane Margaret. It finally made its public debut in 1852 under the title *Canadian Crusoes: A Tale of the Rice Lake Plains*. Reviews were good and the book sold well. The publisher, Hall and Virtue, had paid Catharine £50 for the text and allowed her to retain the copyright. In later years, under the imprints of other publishers, the book became known as *Lost in the Backwoods* and developed a modest momentum that continued into the first few decades of the new century, becoming perhaps Catharine's best-selling book.

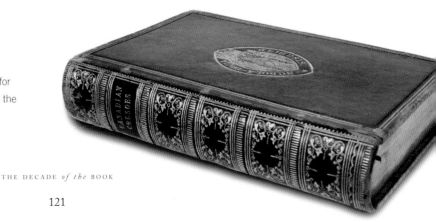

Canadian Crusoes would become a popular success for Catharine, finding favour with young readers well into the twentieth century.

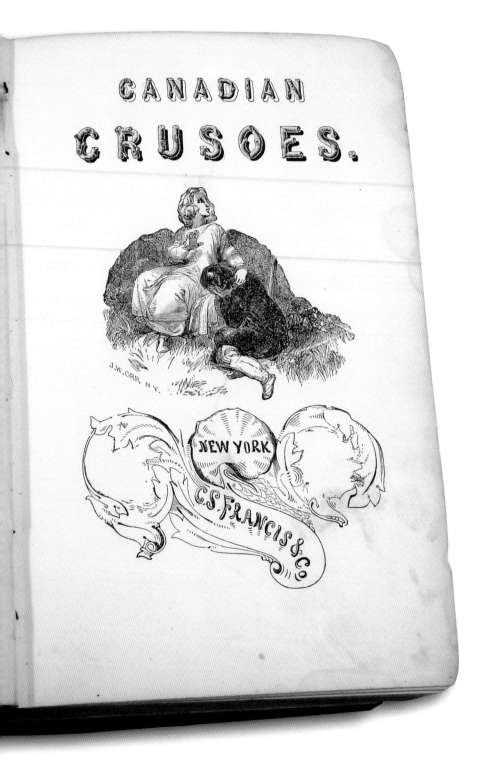

The American edition of *Canadian Crusoes* (left) provided no royalties to Catharine or to its British publisher, though it did use the Biblical-style engravings (above) from the original. Colour illustrations (below) updated the book after it was reissued as *Lost in the Backwoods*.

In *Canadian Crusoes*, Hector and Catharine Maxwell, a brother and sister of Scottish roots, and their French-Canadian cousin Louis meander away from their home while searching for stray cows. The boys are fourteen and Catharine is twelve. Finding themselves utterly lost, they wander north towards the Rice Lake Plains and eventually make a camp for themselves as winter sets in. For two years they survive by relying on their wits and talents, learning much about woodlore from a Mohawk girl who had been left to die in the aftermath of an Indian battle near the lake. The three name her Indiana and undertake to teach her about Christianity. In this regard, *Canadian Crusoes* is a captivity narrative in reverse, a benign tale of survival and conversion. Riding smoothly on a carpet of Victorian optimism, it manifests a faith in the inherent goodness of children, the shepherdly watchfulness of God and the resourcefulness of the British spirit. Catharine also suggests the possible unification of the founding elements of Canadian society with the marriages of the industrious Hector to the beautiful Indiana and of the delicate but durable Catharine to her French-Canadian cousin, Louis.

In addition to writing for *The Anglo-American Magazine*, the busy Catharine was able to publish sketches and stories in numerous magazines in Canada, the United States and Britain. At the same time, she continued to explore various possible outlets through which to publish books.[1] Because income was

Many of Catharine Parr Traill's books were written on this small writing desk that is now in the collection of the Peterborough Centennial Museum.

at the forefront of her thinking, she was desperate enough to accept lesser amounts for her writing than she might have gained had she been more patient or tough-minded. In an 1856 letter, Agnes, little comprehending her sister's impoverished state, complained self-righteously that Catharine had lost a good deal of income by agreeing to Hall and Virtue's offer of £25 for a reprint edition of *Canadian Crusoes*.

Susanna encountered much smoother sailing as she prepared the manuscript of *Roughing It in the Bush* for publication. Richard Bentley, the distinguished London publisher who had issued her husband's memoir of South Africa, agreed to take on the book as a two-volume project and was pleased to learn that Susanna's contributions would be supplemented by pieces from John Moodie and Samuel Strickland.[2] During 1848–49, Susanna focused on the project and completed the sketches needed to fill out the second volume about their time in Douro.

She recopied and altered the Canadian chapters that had already appeared in print, adding appropriate poems by John and herself. However, *Roughing It's* voyage through the publishing process was not entirely smooth. One of the sketches, entitled "Michael McBride," which described Susanna's efforts to provide spiritual comfort to a dying Catholic lad in Cobourg in 1832, met with a hostile response when it appeared in *The Literary Garland*

in February 1851. The Catholic press in Montreal was outraged at her Protestant presumption, a reaction that so alarmed Susanna that she sought to withdraw the piece from the manuscript. Although she hurriedly prepared two new sketches, they arrived in London too late to be inserted into the book.[3]

In the end, the controversy mattered little to reviewers and readers. *Roughing It in the Bush* was a huge success when it appeared in England in February

London publisher, Richard Bentley, had a bestseller in *Roughing It in the Bush* and kept up an active correspondence with its author in letters such as the one at left. (Opposite) The title page of the pirated U.S. edition.

of 1852. The English reviews gave it the kind of praise Susanna might have dreamed of as a young bluestocking in Bloomsbury. It was an adventure story to enthrall gentlemen and gentlewomen alike, a personal account that one literary admirer said was more effective than fiction could ever be. A delighted Richard Bentley quickly authorized a second edition that June.

But one gentlewoman was less than enchanted with the book. Upon receiving an advance copy from Bentley, Agnes Strickland opened it to find that it was dedicated to her as a "simple Tribute of Affection" from her sister. The affection may have been genuine, but Susanna was also astute in gauging the promotional value of her family connection with the now-famous Agnes. She had not, however, foreseen Agnes's anger at being identified with a book about the coarse and common inhabitants of the Canadian backwoods. In a scorching letter, Agnes insisted that her name be removed from all future editions and scolded Susanna for making public her miserable failures as a settler. Agnes also prevailed upon her brother Sam, who was then visiting Reydon, to write a more positive pioneering memoir (*Twenty-Seven Years in Canada West*, published in 1853). She negotiated a princely advance for it — far greater than the one Susanna had received — from Richard Bentley.

Neither advance nor royalties would be paid to Susanna for *Roughing It* in the United States, where it

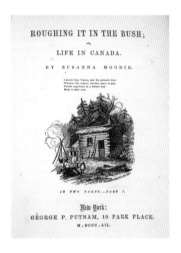

ROUGHING IT IN THE BUSH;
OR,
LIFE IN CANADA.

BY SUSANNA MOODIE.

IN TWO PARTS.—PART I.

New York:
GEORGE P. PUTNAM, 10 PARK PLACE.
M.DCCC.LII.

was published in a pirated edition by George Putnam. Copyright, at the time, pertained only to the country in which the author resided when the book was published.[4] Putnam employed an editor to relieve the text of much of its perceived anti-Americanism and pro-British excesses as well as its poetry, thereby reducing it to a single volume. The strategy proved very effective. So strong were its American sales that Susanna heard reports in 1853 that the book was selling nearly as strongly as the great bestseller of the day, Harriet Beecher Stowe's *Uncle Tom's Cabin*.

Richard Bentley, however, put a value on both Susanna's writing and the friendship they had developed by correspondence. Even before *Roughing It* was printed, he had agreed to publish her novel, *Mark Hurdlestone; or, The Gold Worshipper* (1852). Though the reviews it received were more guarded, it sold reasonably well on the basis of its author's newly-won prominence. Bentley's keenest interest, however, was in a sequel to *Roughing It*, a book that would depict for British readers the burgeoning towns of colonial Canada as opposed to life in the bush. His request arrived in Belleville as Susanna was trying to recover from "one of those painful internal complaints which are generally fatal to all attacked by them." Though she suffered at least two intestinal hemorrhages in 1852, she was able to avoid surgery and decided to travel to Toronto and Niagara Falls early that autumn. An account of

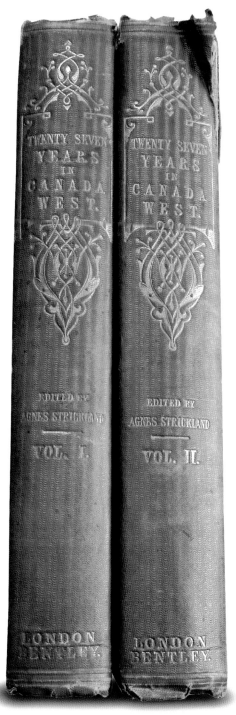

Sam Strickland's *Twenty-Seven Years in Canada West* (left) sold well in England despite its rather stiff prose. The hands-on editing provided by sisters Agnes and Jane Margaret ensured that anything "vulgar" was deleted. For Agnes, this account of Sam's success in Canada helped restore the Strickland family name after the "vexation" caused by *Roughing It in the Bush.*

her journey provided her with a structural device to draw together the sketches for *Life in the Clearings versus the Bush* (1853). Integrating the two belated sketches for *Roughing It* and other previously published material, she turned out a lively and richly descriptive account of life in the developing towns of Canada West that has proved a valuable resource to historians ever since.

By 1854, however, neither *Mark Hurdlestone* nor *Life in the Clearings* was generating sufficient sales to please Bentley. With interest in her work south of the border growing stronger, however, and seeking to head off further piracy, Susanna arranged for the fledgling New York firm of DeWitt and Davenport to publish both books. As hoped, they sold much better in the United States than they had in Britain. She tried to keep up her British publisher's hopes of another bestseller from Canada by providing the texts for *Flora Lyndsay*, the fictionalized prequel to *Roughing It in the Bush*,[5] and *Matrimonial Speculations*, a collection of three novella-length narratives previously published in Canada. Bentley published both books in 1854, while DeWitt and Davenport, who specialized in sentimental and melodramatic fiction and sensational stories of the day, chose to publish only *Flora Lyndsay*, in 1855. However, with Bentley's compliance, the American firm took the lead in publishing *Geoffrey Moncton; or, The Faithless Guardian* (also in 1855), which Bentley brought out a year later under the altered title *The Monctons: A Novel*. With disappointing sales in both markets, however, Susanna Moodie's brief period of competitive demand among publishers in the two countries came to an end. By then, as her letters reveal, so had her energy for authorship.

By mid-decade, Susanna had also grown weary of what she regarded as unrelenting Canadian antagonism towards her bestselling book.[6] She encapsulated her disappointment with Canadian readers in a letter to Richard Bentley in 1856:

> *It is difficult to write a work of fiction, placing the scene in Canada, without rousing up the whole country against me.... Will they ever forgive me for writing* Roughing It? *They know that it was the truth, but have I not been a mark for every vulgar editor of a village journal, through the length and breadth of the land to hurl a stone at, and point out as the enemy of Canada. Had I gained a fortune by that book, it would have been dearly earned by the constant annoyance I have experienced since its publication. If I write about this country again, it shall not be published till my head is under the sod.*

As well, Susanna had to deal with the painful awareness that the book had led to a complete rupture with her sisters back home. To Catharine she wrote in 1853, "from Reydon, I never hear, and suppose I never shall, as my correspondence is to the poor Mamma, whose will to write is perhaps beyond her power."

Catharine's final book of the 1850s also proved a deep disappointment to her, at least commercially. Already disturbed by the short-changing she had experienced from publishers in Canada and England, the pirating of her works in the United States and the chastisement occasionally directed at her by Agnes,

In *Life in the Clearings versus the Bush* (above), Susanna defends herself against some of the criticisms directed at *Roughing It* and attempts to portray a more positive view of Canadian life at mid-century. A chapter on her visit to Kingston Penitentiary, where she saw the "celebrated murderess" Grace Marks, would inspire Margaret Atwood's 1996 novel *Alias Grace*. But neither *Life in the Clearings* nor her two novels, *Geoffrey Moncton* and *Mark Hurdlestone* (left), sold well for her publishers.

The Canadian Settler's Guide

For many immigrant women, adjusting to life in Canada was a hard struggle. In her preface to *The Canadian Settler's Guide*, Catharine describes how the pioneer wife often "toils on heart-sick and pining for the home she left behind her." Having heard women "lament the want of some simple useful book," Catharine decided to share her hard-won knowledge in *The Female Emigrant's Guide and Hints on Canadian Housekeeping*. It first appeared in an inexpensive edition (top) in 1854 and was reissued in expanded form the next year as *The Canadian Settler's Guide* (bottom). The book begins with a complete plan of action for a pioneering family — what supplies are needed and skills required — delivered with small homilies about the virtues of thrift and industry. Practical instructions describe how to roast squirrels and pigeons, brew hemlock tea and treacle beer, braid rag rugs and make candles, and even construct a chair out of a flour barrel. Though the book filled a pressing need and went through many printings, payments to its author were meagre at best.

she entered on her own into an arrangement with the Reverend Henry Hope, an Englishman who had started up a weekly paper in Toronto called *The Old Countryman*. He had sought out Catharine as a contributor by visiting her at Oaklands and asking her to write essays and stories about Canadian domestic life. He could promise no remuneration for the time being, but hoped to be able to do so in the future. Catharine eagerly took up the opportunity and her pieces began to appear on November 2, 1853.

More importantly, she discussed with Hope the manuscript she was preparing as an emigrant's guide for women, a "book such as I should have been glad to have had myself when I came out." The manuscript was a hodgepodge of useful and entertaining information, arranged in part as a seasonal calendar and drawn from a variety of sources: her journals and other manuscripts, articles gleaned from published sources and recipes and household advice submitted to her by friends. She had tried to interest Agnes in selling the book for her, but her sister had been discouraging.[7]

Though only isolated issues of *The Old Countryman* have survived, it is clear that Catharine threw herself into her work for Henry Hope. Writing from Belleville, Susanna was less sanguine about the former minister and his promises, for he had sought her out as well. She saw him as a gabby, self-serving businessman and told her sister, "I can't afford to write for the old twadler for nothing." Still, she watched Catharine's project with interest, sending, at her sister's request, several recipes to include in the volume.

Hope steered *The Female Emigrant's Guide* to completion, though Catharine would later state that she saw no money from the project. The book appeared under two titles — the other being *The Canadian Settler's Guide* — and it went though many "editions" in Canada and in Britain. Over its various printings, little respect was shown for the structure and contents of Catharine's text; parts were simply dropped and replaced with recent data about emigration. Indeed, Hope edited it to fit several emigration projects in which he was involved in the 1860s. He rode the book like a marketable steed, parlaying it into numerous government-based sales and a civil-service position for his son. All the while, he managed to avoid any obligation to its author. Susanna, it would seem, had pegged him correctly: he was a rogue who relied on his former connection to the clergy to give him the stamp of respectability.

Even as Catharine Parr Traill became for many readers, in Charlotte Gray's words, "the Martha Stewart of the backwoods, setting standards of taste and endurance that few other women could achieve," her life bore little relation to the image. She continued to drudge along on the farm at Rice Lake, overburdened with family concerns and financial worries, a sadly exploited victim of the Reverend Henry Hope. Still, despite so many disappointments, she soldiered on, hopeful of better results in the future. In an 1855 letter, she offered what might be taken as her literary credo:

> *The time may come when my name will be associated in the literary history of this new country, and I am more ambitious of its being recorded for the useful than the amusing only.*

Sam Strickland: The Successful Pioneer

Col. Samuel Strickland
Founder of Lakefield

Res. R.L. Strickland,
Lakefield.

Arriving in Upper Canada in 1825, twenty-year-old Sam Strickland settled first in Darlington with family friends named Black, and married their daughter, Emma, in 1826. After Emma died in childbirth that same year, Sam joined John Galt's Canada Company in opening the town sites of Guelph and Goderich. Carefully investing his earnings in land near Peterborough, he traded that property for cash and some land in Douro and was vigorously clearing and farming this property when his sisters arrived in 1832. Sam went on to considerable success as a landowner and lumberman, buying up valuable timber and water rights in the Lakefield area. He ran his farm as an agricultural school for young Englishmen, and this contributed to the genteel social milieu of the town. He also became an officer in the local militia and a justice of the peace. Marrying twice more, Sam fathered fourteen children by his second wife Mary Reid, and died just before Canada West became part of the new Dominion of Canada in 1867.

(Opposite) A white-whiskered Sam stands in front of his Lakefield home, the Homestead, at a family gathering circa 1860. Catharine Parr Traill is seated to the left with some of her nephews. Sam's third wife, Katherine Rackham, stands in the foreground. A view of Lakefield (top) from the same period shows the thriving town it had become. The Homestead (above) burned down in 1913, but Reydon Manor (below), built by Sam's son Robert, is a surviving symbol of Strickland prosperity.

CHAPTER TEN

Changes

IN 1853, A YOUNG SCOTSMAN NAMED GEORGE B. LEITH CAME TO GORE'S Landing in search of good farmland. He sought out Thomas Traill as a local guide, and his description of the visit provides a poignant glimpse of the Traills' life at Oaklands at the time:

The cabin the Traills rented at Mount Ararat is long gone but a rustic fence marks where it once stood. An 1820 painting by Charles Fothergill (above, right) entitled *Log House on the Rice Lake* evokes both Mount Ararat and the Traill farm at Oaklands.

Fancy a tall thin faced man of about fifty, with a long kind of loose great coat of grey cloth a good deal faded and stained — a shawl around his neck that one would not have picked out of the gutter and that had not been washed for a month — a nose very much smeared by snuff, hands and face evidently in want of soap and water yet with all this unprepossessing exterior evidently a kind-hearted and well-informed man and ready and anxious to do all in his power to procure information for me — He has not been fortunate in his farming operations being unfitted both mentally and physically for anything of the kind.... We went up in the evening to see Mrs. Traill and found her an invalid on the sofa busy with manufacturing leaves of some new book she is to publish soon. She is a pleasant enough woman, elderly, stout and with a slightly blue tinge but very frank and made no secret of their having had a great struggle for the bare necessities.[1]

The Traills' "great struggle" would intensify dramatically on August 25, 1857, when they awoke at 3 a.m. to find Oaklands on fire. Struggling desperately to awaken all the children, they got everyone out but managed to save only some items of furniture and a few of Catharine's valued nature manuscripts. Outside in the dark, they watched helplessly as flames consumed the log house. They found shelter at the nearby farm of their young friend Clinton Atwood.

The tragic loss of Oaklands and all their capital — save some of Catharine's writing and the crops in the ground — left them virtually destitute. Now in his early sixties, Thomas was no match for the situation his family had to face. Friends and family members, however, were ready to offer refuge and support, and for the next eighteen months the Traills stayed with Sam Strickland at the Homestead in Lakefield or at Park Cottage, owned by the widowed Frances Stewart. The children were sent to stay with friends or found work and board through family connections.

Of greatest concern to Catharine following the loss of Oaklands was Thomas's health. He was failing noticeably, and his will to live fluctuated with his state of mind. She stayed close by him as much as possible, engaging him in quiet chats, listening and taking notes as he reviewed the untoward twists and turns of his life. At his bedside she learned of his deep disappointment at being made the scapegoat for the failure of

(Opposite) John and Susanna pose with family members in front of their Belleville home in 1866. (Left) The front porch of the Moodie cottage today.

Westove, the once-valuable family estate in the Orkneys. He was too despondent even to attend the wedding of his daughter Annie Traill to Clinton Atwood in the spring of 1858 in Christ Church, Lakefield.

On June 21, 1859, at Park Cottage, Thomas Traill slipped quietly away. Some family members, like Susanna, greeted the news with both sadness and a sense of relief, believing that, regardless of his merits, her sister would be better off without him. Catharine, however, was quietly bereft. She took her loss stoically, but for nearly fifteen years wore widow's black in Thomas's honour and always remembered him fondly as "a true hearted loyal gentleman, faithful in deed and word a kind & benevolent disposition, a loving father, husband & friend, a scholar and a true gentleman, whose virtues will be remembered long after his faults have been forgotten."[2]

In Belleville, a great change for the Moodies came about in a very different and rather exotic way — through their engagement with what Susanna would call the "glorious madness" of Spiritualism. Beginning as skeptics, they nevertheless read with fascination the many newspaper reports about the growing popularity of spirit communication. But it took a personal contact to galvanize their interest. On several occasions in 1854 and 1855 they had the opportunity to meet the likeable Kate Fox in Belleville. Kate had gained considerable notoriety as one of the "Rochester Rappers," a trio of sisters who, it was reported, could communicate with the spirit world through their special sensitivity to rappings they heard during seances. John saw her as "a simple and artless

girl," but to Susanna she was a romantic phenomenon of a beguiling kind, "a very lovely intellectual looking girl, with the most beautiful eyes I ever saw in a human head."[3]

The Fox family had spent considerable time in Canada prior to moving south of the border in the 1840s. A fourth sister had married in Canada and was living in a town near Belleville, where Kate came to visit her on several occasions. In the fall of 1855 she cheerfully introduced John and Susanna to the mysteries of communing with the spirit world. Susanna was particularly impressed when Kate Fox's rappings spelled out the name of her friend Anna Harral, who had died in 1830. "Perhaps no one but myself on the whole American continent knew that such a person had ever existed," she wrote.

Both of the Moodies were in need of something new and engrossing at this time. John's work as sheriff was growing increasingly tiresome because of continuing lawsuits and the constant tedium of work and travel. Susanna's frustrations with her writing grew as the number of her unprofitable publications mounted.[4] Kate Fox initiated them into a practice that spoke powerfully to many aching personal needs. John was the first to cross over, while a skeptical Susanna resisted commitment. This led to several sharp disputes between them as John began to attend seances in the homes of Belleville friends. By 1858, however, Susanna had overcome her resistance and soon proved to be an excellent medium, susceptible to messages from many spirit figures of both a personal and religious nature. John became the secretary-manager, organizing the seances and recording in his "Spiritualist Album"

The Rochester Rappers

The sisters who introduced the Moodies to communication with the spirit world are regarded as founders of the Spiritualist movement. In 1848 the two younger Fox sisters, Kate and Margaret (right, at centre and left) were living with their parents in a house in Hydesville (below), near Rochester, New York. In late March the family began to hear knocking sounds, and Kate eventually challenged the noise-maker to repeat the raps to snaps of her fingers. Before long, a code had been worked out whereby the raps could mean yes or no or spell out words using the letters of the alphabet. Kate was sent away to the home of her sister Leah (right, at right), but the rappings followed her, and soon both sisters were able to make the rapping sounds

Kate Fox

from the spirit world. By November of 1849 the sisters were giving public performances and causing a sensation. With sister Leah they toured and gave seances that became ever more elaborate, with objects mysteriously moving and tables levitating. They were embraced by such luminaries as P.T. Barnum and James Fenimore Cooper, and newspaper editor Horace Greeley invited them to stay at his New York home. Many tests were conducted on the sisters, but fraud was never proven. With fame came heartache — both Kate and Margaret developed drinking problems, and by 1885 Spiritualism was in serious decline. In 1888, with Kate present, Margaret demonstrated to a large audience how she could produce raps by cracking her toe joint. She recanted this in 1889, but within five years both sisters had died, penniless and in disgrace.

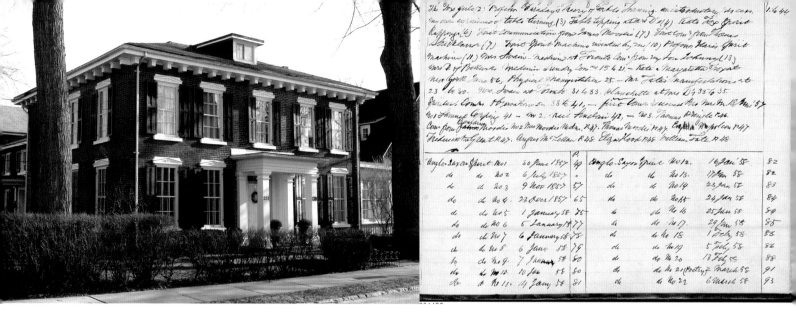

Seances such as the one depicted below were conducted in the homes of a few of Belleville's leading citizens, including that of Mayor John O' Hare (above, left). John meticulously noted each one in his Spiritualist diary (above, right) and also contributed several long articles to the movement's newspaper, the *Spiritual Telegraph* (opposite).

information about participants and the spirit messages received. He even invented a "spiritoscope," a mobile board (rather like a Ouija board on wheels) that allowed for the quicker receipt of spirit messages. In pursuit of contacts, advice and insider news, he travelled frequently to Toronto and to New York City, and in 1858–59 wrote lengthy letters about his personal experiments to the movement's newspaper, the *Spiritual Telegraph*.

Though he longed to be a medium himself, John accepted the reality that he was too rational to be a conduit for spiritual messengers. Susanna, however, reported receiving messages from her father, her son Johnnie, old Suffolk friends and many patriarchal religious voices who would affirm God's perfection, man's vulnerability to various evils and the limitations of human reason. Yet a side of Susanna was always resistant to the movement and kept her unsure of her own commitment. A hesitant Catharine, once initiated by the Moodies, also proved to be an effective medium but was disturbed by certain messages she received. According to Susanna, the spirits sometimes communicated with her in foreign languages and "often abuse[d her], and call[ed] her very ugly names." Still, like her sister, Catharine was comforted by communications with her "dear children." After one spirit-filled visit to the Moodies in 1859, the widowed Catharine left Belleville in a shaken state. Back in Lakefield, her brother Sam convinced her to abandon

the experimentation and, once away from the Moodies' influence, she did.

In the late 1850s, John spent less and less time at his professional duties as he became convinced that he had within him special powers as a healer. Colds, deafness, lameness, even deadly illnesses like cancer could be treated by special "mesmeric passes" of the healer's hands over the ailing parts of the sufferer's body. In his Spiritualist diary, he describes experiments and successes with sufferers who came to him — though, as might be expected, there are few entries on failed attempts. When he suffered a debilitating stroke that rendered him partially lame in 1861, he could find no Spiritualist remedy. His diary entries trail off in 1862 without providing any explanation for their termination. His daughter Katie Vickers, however, added a retrospective note of explanation to the diary — her dear father, she reported, had lived to see the errors underlying his involvement in the movement.

It was only a matter of time before vigilant observers in Belleville noted that John's deputies were doing more and more of his work for him. In 1858 his enemies mounted a case of unprofessional conduct against him based on a charge of "farming of offices." They found the smoking gun in a formal agreement that John had signed, allowing his deputies to perform some of his duties and to draw the related financial rewards. Arguably, such an arrangement may have

"And So My Beloved Rests"

A poignant link to the life of Catharine Parr Traill can be found in a gravestone at St. George's Church in Gore's Landing. Clinton Atwood, a minister's son from Lancashire, came out from England in 1855 on the recommendation of the Rev. George Bridges. He stayed with and worked for the Traills before buying his own farm nearby. In 1858 he married Annie Traill and their first child, Henry Strickland Atwood, was born in 1860, and a daughter, Emily, followed in 1863. But at Christmas of that year, three-year-old Henry came down with chicken-pox, followed by scarlet fever, and died on the night of January 3, 1864. Catharine was present and, as she described in a letter to her old friend Frances Stewart, "I took him away to my own room and left her [Annie] and the poor father to console each other.... I had so often clothed him as an infant and now it was my duty to robe him for the grave.... Clinton and I laid him in the coffin — a bunch of white everlasting was placed in the marble hands, it was an emblem of his new life Immortell — and so my beloved rests."

Two years after Henry's death, the Atwood farmhouse burned to the ground and was replaced in 1867 with a brick house, Atwood Oaks, which still stands today (left). (Top) In 1886 the Atwoods moved to a home they called Ashelworth in Lakefield, and their daughter Annie lived there until her death in 1971, at the age of 100.

been necessary for the elderly and weary sheriff, but it was nonetheless illegal. Convinced he had done no wrong, John was forced into the painful role of passive observer as the case passed through various courts in the province. At each level he met defeat. Hoping against hope to find an effective legal defence — and even, perhaps, an intervention of the spirits on his behalf — he could only watch and wait. He had been advised to trust in public sympathy, which for the most part was on his side. One of his hopes was that the government might create a less stressful form of employment for him, given his age and his health. No less a figure than John A. Macdonald promised to help him. But, finally, in 1863 he resigned his post, a few months before the final verdict against him was passed down in a Toronto court.

Despite his twenty-three years of public service, John had no pension. The Moodies' financial situation was precarious, and they worried about how they might sustain themselves in their old age, let alone provide support for their children. When it came to such practical matters, Spiritualism offered no assistance whatsoever. Their interest by this time had largely waned, in any case, and the movement had been subjected to increasing scrutiny in the press.

In Lakefield, Catharine continued to live on the edge of outright poverty. After Thomas's death she had been able, through monetary gifts and the efforts of Sam Strickland, to purchase a property beside the Otonabee River. Sam organized the building of a frame house for her that was completed in the summer of 1860. To help cover the costs of furnishing and heating it, Catharine and her unmarried daughter Kate rented out the house when they could and boarded with family members. Another daughter, Mary, had begun to teach school in the area and, while living with her mother and sister, would contribute what she could to the household expenses.

Catharine's letters of the early 1860s concentrate on her concern for her children and their prospects. By 1863 she had five grandchildren, three by her eldest son, James, and his wife, Amelia. Daughter Annie had given birth to her second child that year at the Atwood farm on Rice Lake. Annie's uncertain health and the needs of her children drew lengthy visits from both her sister Kate or her mother. Catharine's skill as a midwife meant that she was often called upon to assist at births within her family and in Lakefield.

Susanna's letters at this time fret about their financial situation and the unfairness with which John had been treated. She was increasingly feeling her age as rheumatism affected her limbs and ulcers disturbed her stomach. To Catharine she reported on her weight gain, which she described as "a great change in my physical woman." Death haunted her in numerous ways, particularly in the unexpected return of Jenny Buchanan to their Belleville home in 1862. Like Robert Frost's hired man, the rough-mannered servant who had been Susanna's sole help in her last three years in the bush had come home to die. Two years later, Susanna's mother Elizabeth would pass on at Reydon Hall in her ninety-third year, but even this did not lead to a thawing in the frosty relations between Susanna and her sisters in England.

The Sisters of Southwold

Although Agnes Strickland (at left and right) spent much of her time visiting grand houses as part of her research into royal lives, Reydon Hall remained home for her and Jane Margaret until their mother's death in 1864. (Eliza lived alone in a village cottage in Surrey, and the widowed Sarah had married Richard Gwillym, a vicar from the Lake District, in 1844.) Jane had managed to save enough money from her writing to purchase a house in Southwold. After the sale of Reydon Hall, she leased Park Cottage to Agnes and moved into a small annex connected by a door. (When sisterly quarrels erupted, this door was reportedly slammed and locked.) Though Agnes's relationship with Eliza was also frequently stormy, they agreed to collaborate yet again on a royal biography series, this time about Tudor princesses, published in 1867. Jane Margaret assisted on another book about the Stuart princesses, which followed in 1871. Two years later, Agnes suffered a fall and then a stroke and died the following summer at the age of seventy-eight.

(Opposite) A studio photograph and an engraving, both from the late 1860s, depict Agnes Strickland as the rather formidable figure she undoubtedly was. Agnes would die in 1874 at Park Cottage, and a plaque on the garden wall remembers her. Ivy has almost overgrown her tombstone in St. Edmund's churchyard (below, at right.) A headstone for Jane Margaret, who died in 1888, stands beside it.

CHAPTER ELEVEN

National Treasures

THE FINAL CHAPTERS IN THE LIVES OF THE CANADIAN Strickland sisters were rather quiet and often sad. While the Moodies struggled with the loss of John's position and the legal costs associated with his various trials, they were helped financially by their son-in-law John Vickers. They also took in boarders — two sisters from Jamaica who had come to Belleville in 1860 on the recommendation of the Reverend George Bridges. The Russell girls, Eliza and Julia, provided a youthful presence in the house, and to Susanna they were "a special comfort." Eventually, they married the two eldest Moodie boys — Dunbar wed Eliza in 1862, and Donald married Julia four years later.

But this positive change in the Moodie household would turn sour within a few years. Once married, Eliza and Dunbar wanted to try their luck in the United States. They were drawn first to a farm in Delaware and then to the newly-opened American west, and they encouraged Susanna and John to join them in their experiment. Unwisely, John transferred ownership of the Belleville house to his eldest son, only to have Dunbar sell it as a means of financing his scheme. A prolonged debacle ensued. In Toronto, Katie and John Vickers were outraged by the sale because it deprived her parents of their major equity. Then, faced with the unattractive reality of a move, the Moodies refused to leave Belleville. John's health was not strong after his stroke and, characteristically,

(Opposite) The Moodies pose affectionately with Eliza Russell on the steps of the Moodie cottage. Eliza and her sister Julia would later earn the Moodies' animosity when they became daughters-in-law. (Above) The Moodie cottage today.

The main staircase and
doorway at the Moodie cottage.

Susanna found herself unwilling to leave her home of nearly twenty-five years. Family tensions increased as the frustrated Vickerses cut off communication with Susanna and John.

Susanna directed much of her anger at Eliza, who passed quickly from saint to arrogant sinner in her mind. When Dunbar and Eliza headed south with their two young children in 1865, the Moodies stayed behind and rented a small cottage near the bay. With their diminished resources there was little they could do for their daughter Agnes when her husband, Charles Fitzgibbon, died in 1865, leaving her with six children to support. Nor could they do much to help the unsteady Donald after he married Julia Russell in New York in 1866 without their knowledge or approval. Their youngest son, Robert, married a Belleville girl named Nellie Russell (no relation) in 1863 and stayed close by. Happy as ever in their marriage, the Moodies found comfort in their new and simpler life together; they had a dog, a cat and a cow, along with hens at the door, and only a modest rent to pay.

Briefly, too, they returned to writing as a way of supporting themselves. Susanna turned once again to her loyal friends in the publishing business, John Lovell in Montreal and Richard Bentley in London. She wrote a long novel for Lovell, which was serialized in his new paper, the Montreal *Daily News*, in 1867 under the title of "Dorothy Chance." Though the story was set in England, Susanna considered it a Confederation narrative of a kind, Dorothy's initials carrying the code of the new Dominion. She then sent the printed newspaper text to Bentley, who published it in London as a three-volume novel in 1868 under the title *The World Before Them*.

John gathered many of his occasional pieces together in a volume called *Scenes and Adventures as a Soldier and Settler, During Half a Century* (1866). Travelling to Montreal with Susanna, he arranged with John Lovell to publish the book by subscription and had his picture taken by photographer William Notman for its frontispiece. Happily, the little book did well for the Moodies, producing a profit of some $600, a sum that could have supported them for a year had it not gone to pay off their debts. It was a tribute to the esteem in which many friends and associates held him that the sales were so strong. Nostalgic for his Orkney roots, John also wrote several pieces about Norse and Orcadian history and family genealogy for a Kirkwall newspaper, the *Orkney Herald*.

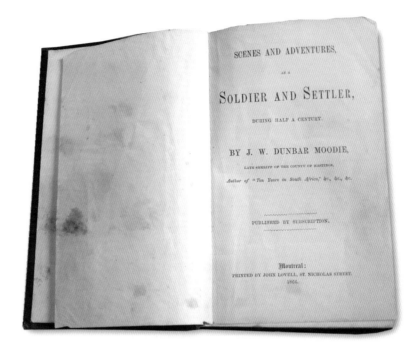

Despite his failing eyesight, John Moodie edited this collection of past writings and published them with a new introduction recalling his life and career.

Richard Bentley never forgot how much money he had earned from Susanna's best writing, and in appreciation he arranged for her to receive a grant in 1865 from the Royal Literary Fund, of which he was a director. Designed to provide support for British writers in untoward circumstances, the fund proved a godsend to the Moodies. This grant of £60 ($300) was the only one Susanna received as a writer during her lengthy career.

It is likely that Susanna found more satisfaction from painting than writing during these years. She found a market for her watercolour representations of flowers with an appropriate poem glued to the back of the picture. These she sold for as much as five pounds apiece in bookstores in Montreal, Toronto and Belleville, and a number of them can be found today in museums around the country.

The domestic quiet of the Moodies' retirement lasted until the early morning of October 22, 1869, when Susanna's "dear old Norseman" passed away in their cottage at the age of seventy-three. Susanna mourned his loss deeply. In a letter to one of John's friends, she noted that "he had one of the largest funerals ever known here which reached from our cottage to the English church a full mile in length. Even the

"And so we parted and though I was with him till the last and held the dear hand long after it was cold, he never was able to say words of love or tenderness to me again."

men whose persecutions had shortened his days paid respect to his remains." Replying to a letter of condolence from the County Council of Hastings, she noted pointedly, "I have *indeed*, lost an excellent husband, endeared to me by his many domestic virtues, and a *just, honest* man, has passed away from your midst."

Besides his grieving widow, John Moodie left behind five surviving children and twenty grandchildren.

The remaining years of Susanna's life passed by sedately, with scarcely a literary ruffle — a poem here and a sketch there. In the summers she often accepted Catharine's invitation to spend a month with her at her Lakefield cottage. On one holiday outing, Susanna had the opportunity to take a pleasure cruise on the *Chippewa*, a steamer piloted by her nephew, Percy

Strickland. Sailing north on Lake Katchewanook, they passed by her old homestead in the Douro wilderness. "[T]he scenery I once knew along the shores was quite changed," she observed. "Our old place I should never have recognized. The woods about it are all gone, and a new growth of small cedar fringes the shore in front. There is a tolerable looking modern cottage on the spot that the old log house once occupied, and the old barn survives on the same spot on which it was built, more than 30 years ago, but the woods that framed it in, are all down, and it has a bare desolate look."

As she watched the shoreline of Clear Lake give way to Stony Lake, she was awed once again by the "grand scenery" and "labyrinth of islands" before her: "It is a wonderful place, so vast, so wild and lonely, the

The last photographs taken of John and Susanna Moodie are these 1866 portraits by Notman of Montreal.

As a widow, Susanna depended most on her youngest son, Rob — seen above with his wife, Nellie, and one of their seven children — and on her eldest daughter, Catherine Vickers, pictured below with her large family.

waters so blue, the dark woods frowning down upon them from their lofty granite ridges that towered far far above us." She concluded with the accurate prophecy, "The time will come when this will be one of the sight seeing places in Canada."

Heartened by the renewed attentions of the Vickerses and the steady interest of her youngest son, Rob, she closed up the cottage and, after briefly boarding on her own in Belleville, moved back and forth from one of her children's homes to the other. Despite a large and growing family, the Vickers were better able to make her comfortable in their large Adelaide Street house. John, who had founded the Vickers Northern Express Company and served as a Toronto alderman, was much better off than the hard-working Rob.[1] The one literary project that Susanna was happy to undertake occurred in 1870 while she was living in Seaforth, where Rob was the stationmaster for the Grand Trunk Railroad. Approached by the Toronto publishing firm of Hunter, Rose and Company to prepare a Canadian edition of *Roughing It in the Bush*, she undertook some minor revisions and wrote a new introduction entitled "Canada: A Contrast." Reviews were more positive than they had been twenty years before. Now more manageable in a single volume, it was seen as "an extremely lively book, full of incident and character" and "by no means a jeremiad."

Widowhood seemed to agree with her sister Catharine and, though there was always a struggle to meet the costs of living in the cottage (now named Westove in honour of Thomas Traill's Orkney home), she settled into a productive routine there. Kate ran the household effectively, and between them they made up albums of dried flowers and ferns as gifts and sale items. A mid-1860s visit to her niece Agnes Fitzgibbon in Toronto led to a new project of great interest to Catharine. The two agreed to combine their skills and energies on an illustrated book about Canadian wildflowers. Agnes learned lithography in order to produce plates of flower drawings that could be hand-coloured, while Catharine wrote texts for the plates. The result was a handsome book sold by subscription and suitable for prominent display in one's parlour. *Canadian Wild Flowers* was published by John Lovell in 1868 in an edition of five hundred copies, many of them hand-painted by Agnes and her children. So successful was the first edition that three others followed (1869, 1870 and 1895).

As the 1860s gave way to the '70s, Catharine continued in her role as dutiful and supportive matriarch. Losses and sadness were inevitable, and in her seventh decade she buried two of her children and saw her two youngest sons depart for western Canada, scarcely to be seen again.[2] The news of the murder of her eldest son, thirty-three-year-old Hal, in Kingston in 1870 was a particularly heavy blow. On duty as a guard at the penitentiary, he was killed by two prisoners during an escape attempt. Catharine had always lamented Hal's lack of educational opportunities and had closely followed his struggles to find work to support his wife and three children. Catharine and Katie soon adopted three-year-old Katharine Parr, Hal's only daughter, and so Westove became home to three Kates — mother, daughter and granddaughter — for much of the next two decades.

Another death that loomed particularly large for Catharine was that of Frances Stewart in 1872 at the age of seventy-eight. The loss *(continued on p. 155)*

Susanna's second daughter, Agnes (right), was left with little support when her husband, Charles Fitzgibbon, died in 1865. But she had considerable skills with a paintbrush and decided to work with her Aunt Catharine, and illustrate her manuscript on Canadian wildflowers. The title page of their collaboration is shown below.

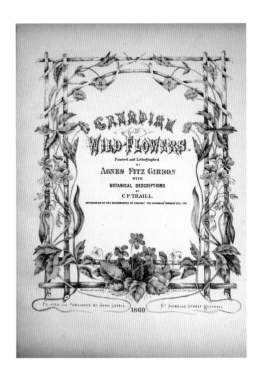

Canadian Wild Flowers

The publication of *Canadian Wild Flowers* in 1868 was greeted with almost universal praise. The *Montreal Daily News* hailed it as "a most valuable addition to the literature of Canada." No reviewers commented, however, on the fact that Agnes Fitzgibbon received a more prominent billing on the book's title page than did its well-known author, Mrs. Traill. Although the text incorporates Catharine's botanical knowledge gained from over thirty years of collecting Canadian specimens in her scrapbooks (far left) and sometimes preserving them with her flower press (right), the book was made a reality by her niece's tireless efforts. It was Agnes who persuaded John Lovell in Montreal to publish the book and then spearheaded the subscription drive to find 500 buyers for it (at the then-high price of five dollars per copy). And it was Agnes who engraved ten floral designs on a lithography stone and ran off 500 copies of each. She then enlisted her three daughters to join her in hand-colouring all 5,000 illustrations for the first edition of the book, and devoted much of 1867 to shepherding it through publication. Though the book did not earn Agnes a lot of money, it did solve her financial problems. While selling subscriptions in Ottawa, she was introduced to a successful lawyer and member of Parliament, Colonel Brown Chamberlin, and within a year they were married.

AQUILEGIA CANADENSIS
(Wild Columbine)

2 TRILLIUM GRANDIFLORUM
(Large white Trillium)

3 ERYTHRONIUM AMERICANUM
(Yellow adders tongue)

Westove, the frame house where Catharine lived for the last thirty-nine years of her life, still stands above the banks of the Otonabee in Lakefield today.

left her deeply nostalgic for her early days in the bush, when Frances had served as her mentor. Her subsequent correspondence with Frances's daughter, Ellen Dunlop, led to Catharine suggesting that she gather the letters Frances had written home to Ireland for possible publication. Years later, the selected letters, edited by Ellen, were published under the title *Our Forest Home* (1889).

Conditions at Westove had improved considerably over the years. In a letter of January 1861, Catharine described herself as having less than five dollars to her name, but by the late 1870s she and the two Kates were quite comfortable. Money and help had come from many sources, often from immediate family and friends, but the biggest boosts had come in bequests. First there was her share of the inheritance from her mother's estate in 1864 and from the sale of Reydon Hall the following year. Then came the news that she was heir to some of her sister Agnes's estate after her death in England in 1874. Agnes bequeathed the copyrights for *Lives of the Queens of England* to Catharine and her nephew Percy Strickland. (This greatly displeased her sister Eliza, since she had more than earned her share of the rights, but with her death a year later, the money eventually made its way to Lakefield.) There was nothing, however, in Agnes's will for Susanna. Her anger over *Roughing It in the Bush* extended to the grave.[3]

Catharine's own writing continued sporadically

Catharine Parr Traill

during these years. She wrote short pieces for magazines and tried to help her daughter Mary find publishing opportunities. However, it was not until Agnes Fitzgibbon approached her about a second collaboration that she became passionately engaged in a new large-scale project. Agnes had remarried in 1870 (with her proud mother, Susanna, present), and her new husband was Colonel Brown Chamberlin, a lawyer, militia officer and member of Parliament who had been appointed the Queen's Printer in Ottawa. Agnes and her children soon joined him in the new capital, where the couple often entertained at their comfortable home in New Edinburgh. Through Ottawa's new Field Naturalists' Club, Agnes befriended James Fletcher, the young sub-librarian of the Parliamentary Library and the future botanist of the Central Agricultural Farm. With her influential new Ottawa connections, she was well positioned to undertake negotiations with publishers for a new book, to be entitled *Studies of Plant Life in Canada*. Although Catharine had notes on Canadian trees, grasses and shrubs drawn from over fifty years of observation, work on the book was still demanding. But it brought Catharine back in touch with botanist James Macoun, whom she had met in Belleville, and gave her the great pleasure of a new and supportive friend in James Fletcher. It also led to her one and only trip to Ottawa, in the winter of 1884, to work closely with Agnes on the final manuscript and to see some of the sights of the capital.

Several letters provide a record of the visit. There were trips to Parliament and its "Great Library," and to Rideau Hall by invitation from the viceregal couple, Lord and Lady Lansdowne. She also had the pleasure of meeting Prime Minister John A. Macdonald while he was entertaining two Native leaders from the Northwest and the celebrated missionary Father Albert Lacombe in the Parliamentary Library. Lacombe made her very proud when he told her that he knew her sons, and recalled meeting Willie at Lac la Biche.

The letters also report on a rare occasion of public attention during a well-attended winter soiree at Rideau Hall. Catharine was astounded to notice that people were milling around her at the reception, apparently trying to catch a glimpse of the famous author. To Ellen Dunlop she wrote: "The only thing that I did not like was that when I was left in the tearoom every body kept staring at me, and some edged nearly up to me, and I kept hearing — 'That's her — That's Mrs. Traill — ' and so on, and short people stood on tiptoe, and others peered over shoulders and pushed those before them aside peering at poor me as if I had been the shew piece of the play ... not being accustomed to be gazed at in that way   it was a little oppressive."

At one time, Catharine would have eagerly described her Ottawa experiences in letters to Susanna. But by 1884 Susanna was no longer capable of reading them; she had been rendered childlike by a disease that was likely a form of dementia or Alzheimer's. Letters that Catharine wrote during her visit to Toronto in March of 1885 provide our most vivid glimpse of Susanna in her final months. In them, she marvelled at the way in which Katie Vickers was able to provide care and to cater to her mother's vagaries and ramblings. To

Studies of Plant Life in Canada was published in 1885, seventeen years after *Canadian Wild Flowers*. Catharine's niece Agnes once again created the illustrations, although this time the printer added the colour. In her introduction, Catharine described how forest plants had been like dear friends to her and how she regretted their disappearance "as civilization extends through the Dominion."

The Toast of Ottawa

"I am enjoying myself very much," Catharine wrote to her sister Sarah on January 29, 1884, "for all are so good and loving to the old auntie and I am paid more attention to here in Ottawa than I have ever been … my name is now well known and my work valued far more than ever they were." With her niece Agnes now married to the Queen's Printer, Colonel Chamberlin, Catharine was given invitations by "the heads of the society of the place." The grandest occasion of all was a winter soiree at Rideau Hall hosted by the viceregal couple, Lord and Lady Lansdowne. A huge bonfire on the grounds illuminated the toboggans flashing by on the giant slide and Lady Lansdowne took Catharine's arm for a walk to see the skaters spinning to Viennese waltzes on the torch-lit rink. Inside Rideau Hall, a lavish supper was laid on, and Catharine noted how liberally some of the guests took advantage of the hospitality. She felt self-conscious with the attention paid to her at the party but, fortunately, she soon connected with botanist James Fletcher, then sub-librarian of the Parliamentary Library, and the best part of the evening was spent chatting with him about plants and her new manuscript.

(Above, left) Guests at the Rideau Hall winter party pose in front of the "rustic" log cabin which Catharine found to be handsomely panelled inside, not at all like the ones she had once lived in. On a visit to the "Great Library" in the Parliament Buildings (above, right), she was greeted very cordially by Sir John A. Macdonald (right), who was with the Jesuit Père Lacombe and two Indian chiefs, one of whom "was in a fine scarlet uniform, epaulettes and all."

"We watched beside her till rest and peace came and all was over."

Ellen Dunlop she reported on Susanna's state of mind: "What a strange change — what a wreck. Do you know, dear, that my sister who used to rail against dolls and call them hideous idols ... has a great wax doll dressed like a baby and this she nurses and caresses and believes it is her own living babe, and cannot bear it out of her sight.... This is to me the saddest sight for it shows the entire change that has come over her fine intellect.... Poor dear old sister. Well thank God she is unconscious of it herself."

A few weeks later Susanna slipped into a coma with Catharine at her bedside. "We watched beside her," Catharine wrote to her daughter Annie, "till rest and peace came and all was over." Rob Moodie arranged for her body to be taken to Belleville and interred in the new cemetery overlooking the Bay of Quinte. Her husband and two sons were moved from the old cemetery to lie beside her, and a handsome marble angel was erected on the plot. Newspaper obituaries saluted Susanna's achievements, with the Toronto *Globe* accurately hailing her best-known book as a work that would last long after the world she described had disappeared.

After Susanna's death, Catharine was looked after by Kate. She spent most of her time either at Westove or at Kate's rustic cottage, Minnewawa, on a Stony Lake island some fifteen miles to the north. But even as she entered into her nineties she was eager to undertake further projects from among the many partial manuscripts she had written and accumulated over the years. She had done sketches of family members for a Strickland volume with the working title *Memorials: The Stricklands, A Family Chronicle, by an Octogenarian — One of Them.* Jane Margaret had published

The Moodie grave site in Belleville.

158

a glowing biography of the great Agnes in 1887, but had left out the rest of the family (except for Eliza) in her sycophantic account. Catharine hoped to restore a due balance to the family record by commemorating the lives and achievements of the Canadian Stricklands and in celebrating the places (Stowe House, Reydon Hall and Norwich) where the sisters' love of writing had been nurtured.

The death of her daughter Mary Muchall in May 1892 set Catharine back for many months but added urgency to her attempt to preserve her own family's early life. She also had great hopes that she might live to see a first Canadian edition of *The Backwoods of Canada*, as Susanna had been able to do with *Roughing It in the Bush* in 1871. To that end, she carefully worked through a copy of the 1836 edition of her book, adding information about the many changes she

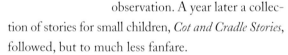
Katherine Traill

had seen in Canada since her arrival in 1832. Kate helped her by typing out many of the longer changes and gluing them into relevant positions in the text. Catharine would dangle this project before family, friends and publishers in the 1890s, but to no immediate avail. It would not appear until thirty years after her death, when it was edited for McClelland & Stewart by Edward S. Caswell, whom Catharine had met through her great-niece, Mary Agnes Fitzgibbon.

Mary Agnes, an heir to the Strickland writing gene, had come to live in Lakefield in 1890 while working on a biography of her famous grandfather,

A Veteran of 1812: The Life of James Fitzgibbon (1894). Her editor at the Methodist Book and Publishing House was the young Edward Caswell, who was delighted to be invited to Westove to meet the venerable Mrs. Traill. Mary Agnes showed him some of her great-aunt's manuscripts, and he was most engaged by the descriptions of plant and bird life that she had written for young readers. Caswell proposed that Mary Agnes work with Catharine on a collection entitled *Pearls and Pebbles, or Notes of an Old Naturalist*, which appeared in December 1894, winning immediate attention and praise in both Canada and England. Principal George Grant of Queen's University and the outspoken journalist and academic Goldwyn Smith wrote glowingly of Catharine's sympathetic style and keen powers of observation. A year later a collection of stories for small children, *Cot and Cradle Stories*, followed, but to much less fanfare.

Though Catharine's opportunities faded with her level of energy over the last four years of her life, she increasingly became a figure of public attention. The new Historical Society of Peterborough named her its honorary president at a special gathering in 1896, but the occasion proved uncomfortable for her because of her deafness and swollen feet and the heat in the hall. She knew better than to appear in public again and, citing her age and poor health, turned down an invitation to meet Lady Aberdeen, the wife of the governor general, whom she much admired.

Other tributes reached her in quiet Lakefield. From England the author Emma Hubbard, a cousin of Clinton Atwood, arranged for her to receive an award of £150 from the Royal Literary Fund. In Canada, her old friend Sir Sandford Fleming, who in the 1840s had begun his impressive engineering career from the Peterborough home of his uncle, John Hutchison, the Traills' doctor, took up a subscription in her name. He persuaded the Dominion of Canada to grant her $1,000 and a small island named Polly

Cow in Lake Katchewanook, north of her original backwoods log house. This gift of the nation, a public recognition of her "literary services" to the country, pleased her very much.[4] The citation presented to her by Sir Sandford Fleming tried to capture her remarkableness as an individual:

You have been instrumental … in leading many
to love the treasures of Nature … which you have
so faithfully portrayed in the Flora and Fauna
of our woods and forests.… We cannot forget the

During her last summer of 1899, Catharine sits on the porch of Minnewawa on Stony Lake with (from left) her daughter Kate, and granddaughters Katy and Ethel.

In a series of letters to Catharine, Sir Sandford Fleming describes his efforts to have Polly Cow Island in Lake Katchewanook (opposite, at centre) ceded to her. In the last letter, he addresses it to "Mrs Catharine Parr Traill of Polly Cow Island, Lakefield."

courage with which you endured the privations and trials of the backwoods in the early settlement of Ontario, and we rejoice to know that your useful life has been prolonged in health and vigour until you now are now the oldest living author in Her Majesty's dominion.

Such praise must have been as welcome to Catharine as the $1,000 that accompanied it. What would have pleased her most, as Fleming well knew, was the tribute to her usefulness. Unlike Susanna, ever sharp-edged and opinionated, ever inclined to soar in her enthusiasms and passions, Catharine remained down to earth, practical and caring. Lucid to the end, it might even be said that she died with a pen in her hand, for she was writing a letter when she collapsed at Minnewawa, passing away two days later at Westove on August 29, 1899.

The deaths of Susanna Moodie and Catharine Parr Traill closed an era in early Canadian writing. Both had become daughters of the country "by adoption," to use Susanna's phrase, and both were delighted to see literary and artistic impulses finding expression in some of their children. More than a century later, their writing has held its own against the best of other early writers. *Roughing It in the Bush* is a staple of Canadian university literature courses in the early twenty-first century, while Catharine's *The Backwoods of Canada* and *Canadian Crusoes* continue to find audiences among specialists and general readers alike. Their books provide disparate views of the experience of settling a new land, meeting its original inhabitants and being part of a new society in the making.

Notes

1) Thomas Strickland's first wife was Susanna Butt, a great-niece of scientist Sir Isaac Newton; but she died in 1790, a few months after their marriage. Three years later, at the age of thirty-five, Thomas married twenty-one-year-old Elizabeth Homer, who is described by Agnes's biographer, Una Pope-Hennessy, as "a gentle, self-effacing woman."

2) Thomas was of farming stock, and his claim to noble lineage through the Stricklands of Sizergh Castle in Cumbria is dubious. Agnes, however, made much of it during her career as a biographer of the queens of England. The Stricklands of Sizergh were granted lands in Lincolnshire by Henry II in 1170–80. Through this family, Thomas asserted kinship to Catherine Parr, the sixth and last wife of Henry VIII, after whom his second-youngest daughter was named. But even for the Stricklands of Sizergh, the connection to Catherine Parr was a distant one, by marriage only.

{ CHAPTER TWO }

1) Agnes dedicated the latter book to Mrs. Leverton "with every sentiment of admiration [to] her affectionate relative."

2) As an aspiring artist, Cheesman had trained in Italy with the celebrated engraver Francesco Bartolozzi (1725–1815) and was an advocate of all things Italian, even to the point of becoming a Catholic. During her visits to Newman Street, Agnes was able to develop a sufficient grasp of Italian to translate a number of Italian poems by Tasso and others for Henry Colburn's *New Monthly Magazine*.

3) Likely the "E" was a typo, for Eliza was uninterested in such writing. An advertisement in *Disobedience* called attention to the error. It listed two other works by the author, Catharine Parr Strickland, as currently "in press": a story entitled "The Alpine, or Fair of Altorf" and a book, *Reformation: or, The Cousins* (James Woodhouse, 1819).

4) The Black family were London-based friends of the Stricklands who crossed the Atlantic to try their luck in the Darlington area of Upper Canada. Samuel Strickland joined them in 1825 and married Emma, one of James Black's daughters. She died in childbirth in 1826.

{ CHAPTER FIVE }

1) Doubtless the church was Anglican; as far as Catharine's family was concerned, she felt that there was no need to specify its denomination, even though Cobourg could also claim a Methodist church and Academy.

2) There was a caricaturist of comic propensities in Susanna's creative nature, a blend of George Cruickshank (whom she had met in London) and Charles Dickens, both of whom she greatly admired.

3) The Moodies weren't sure what Joe Harris would do to them if the law were called in on their behalf. Complacently, Charles Clark advised caution. The fact was that frontier justice was very much the order of things in many parts of Hamilton Township in 1832, as Susanna's sharp and testy observations in "The Charavari" chapter of *Roughing It in the Bush* make clear.

4) During this winter, the Moodies were also preyed upon by the borrowing habits of their "Yankee" neighbours, a practice Susanna demythologizes in *Roughing It in the Bush*.

5) In 1834 N.H. Baird completed a survey of the areas adjacent to the Otonabee water system, and the government had been encouraged to invest in locks and improvements that would increase development and improve transportation.

6) Frances Stewart (1794–1872) had been raised under strict genteel standards in Ireland and could claim strong family connections with the Edgeworths of County Longford, including the well-known author Maria Edgeworth.

7) Though there is no precise mention of her return to Auburn in surviving documents, Catharine's retrospective comments imply several stays with the Stewarts.

8) She joked that the portraits of Lafayette, Kosciusco, Fox and Brougham made for "somewhat radical company" on the walls of their comfortable parlour.

9) Thomas had not yet had sufficient time to find bush life dreadfully isolating and dispiriting, since during their first sixteen months he continued to enjoy ready access to the society of Peterborough-area people like Ephraim Sanford, Dr. John Hutchison and the Reverend Richard D'Olier.

{ CHAPTER SIX }

1) The flood of emigration into Canada had peaked and slackened after 1834, in part because of the persistent threat of cholera and the lure of free land in the United States.

{ CHAPTER SEVEN }

1) Fothergill's full encomium said: "Thanks to the sweet poetess who has so often delighted us from her nesting place in the dark-brown woods of the Newcastle District on subjects of softer interest: and who now shews with what skill she can strike a bolder strain — Yes: all who see it, must thank thee, sweet. Poetess — Daughter of Genius — and, Wife of the Brave."

2) The poems were "On Reading the Proclamation Delivered by William Lyon Mackenzie, on Navy Island" (17 January 1838), "The Banner of England" (24 January 1838), "The Wind That Sweeps Our Native Sea" (25 April 1838) and "The Burning of the *Caroline*" (October 1838). Susanna was also aware that John had given Fothergill a copy of her 1831 book, *Enthusiasm, and Other Poems*, and that he was drawing on her earlier patriotic poems to bolster her fresh contributions.

3) It had taken four long years to complete the sale of the Traill farm; it was likely a function of Thomas's desperation that he was willing to accept £170 cash and a yearly payment of £40 from the new owners, in spite of the much larger amount he had invested in the property and the clearing of some of the land. "Their ill luck appears, poor things, upon the turn," noted Susanna.

4) Susanna wrote, "Every object had become endeared to me during my long exile from civilised life. I loved the lonely lake, with its magnificent belt of dark pines sighing in the breeze; the cedar-swamp, the summer home of my dark Indian friends; my own dear little garden, with its rugged snake-fence which I had helped Jenny to place with my own hands, and which I had assisted the faithful woman in cultivating for the last three years, where I so often braved the tormenting musquitoes [sic], black-flies, and intense heat, to provide vegetables for the use of the family."

{ CHAPTER EIGHT }

1) Initially, John came forward with the required support from two Douro figures: his brother-in-law Sam Strickland and Thomas A. Stewart, who had been a member of the Legislative Assembly in the late 1830s. The judge refused to

accept Strickland, claiming he was unknown to him, and rejected two other nominees, thus forcing John to turn to two River Trent (Trenton) men, Sheldon Hawley and Adam Henry Meyers, whom he knew from his paymaster's work.

2) To make matters worse, the ever-generous Thomas had backed a loan for a fellow Scot named George MacDougall who was building a mill on the Otonabee River north of the Stewart's home. Sadly, MacDougall drowned in the river in 1844, leaving his own young family in desperate need. Despite his own problems, Thomas felt duty-bound to honour his commitment as best he could. With that telling blow, the Traills' time in the Peterborough area reached its nadir. Their only income was Thomas's half-pay pension and occasional money from Catharine's writing.

3) While there were numerous instances of violence across the province during the 1842 election, the press paid particularly close attention to Belleville because of Baldwin's controversial candidacy and the many threats of party hostility.

4) In a letter to her husband in January 1839 she rapturously praised "sweet little Johnnie": "Surely my dear love," she wrote, "I have bought this boy at a great price. He ought to be my best child. You would not know him, he is grown such a fine creature, and laughs, and capers, and crows, and is the most lively babe I ever had."

5) A favourite family story concerned a visit to their home by Chief Justice John Beverly Robinson during the fall of 1843 or spring of 1844. John Moodie reported that Robinson "overheard some remarks we were making as to the effect *that* dreaded name might produce on his conservative nerves." Intrigued by the whispering but puzzled as to its purport, Robinson asked young Johnnie the name of the baby. His answer was wonderfully coy for a five-year-old — "we sometimes call him Robert," he said.

6) In a February 6, 1845, letter to Robert Baldwin, John was apologetic for abandoning "the great principle of Responsible Government" in the public forum, and wrote, "at the age of nearly 50 with a large family entirely dependant on the paltry office I hold for bread, and unable to cloth[e] them as well as respectable mechanics can do — I think you can hardly blame me if I endeavour *at last* to take some care of myself."

{ CHAPTER NINE }

1) Twelve instalments of "The Governor's Daughter; or, Rambles in the Canadian Forest," published in a Toronto magazine, *The Maple Leaf* (1852–53), eventually became the basis for *Lady Mary and Her Nurse; or, A Peep into the Canadian Forest*. Published by Arthur, Hall and Virtue in London in 1856, the book was aimed at a still-younger audience than *Canadian Crusoes*. Like its predecessor, it went through numerous editions with various publishers. In New York and Boston it was pirated and published under the more egalitarian title, *Stories of the Canadian Forest; or, Little Mary and Her Nurse*.

2) The Moodies had enlisted one of John's old Scottish friends, John Bruce, to negotiate with Bentley and to see the manuscript through the press on their behalf. It was only in the wake of Bruce's ill health shortly after *Roughing It in the Bush* was initially published that Susanna was prompted to write directly to Richard Bentley; thereupon began a long and respectful correspondence between the two that Susanna found particularly satisfying.

3) The two replacement sketches were "Jeanie Burns" and "Lost Children."

4) As a British colonial, Moodie had no say about republications of her works in the American marketplace. They were simply in her words "stolen brooms."

5) *Flora Lyndsay* is a fictionalized account of Susanna's life up to emigration. As she told Bentley in an 1853 letter, "This should have been the commencement of *Roughing It*, for it was written for it, and I took a freak of cutting it out of the MS. and beginning the work at Grosse Ile."

6) It is difficult now to trace that plethora of village editors who hurled verbal stones at Susanna, but we do know that Charles Lindsay, in his capacity as the newly-appointed editor of the Toronto *Leader*, called her book a "most mischievous" novel and labelled her "an ape of the aristocracy, too poor to lie on a sofa and too proud to labour for a living." Remembering the grim reality of much of her bush experience, Moodie laughed at that sally, claiming that she was "too much amused to be angry." The accumulation of abuse, however, became too much for her as year piled on year.

7) The excitement in London over the Crimean War had reduced interest in things literary, Agnes reported, but likely she was still very angry with Susanna and, indeed, with the very idea of Canada. Both she and Eliza were sometimes unkind to Catharine in their letters, discouraging her publishing hopes and chastising her for her naiveté; more sympathetically, Jane Margaret sent along several of her Reydon recipes for inclusion.

{ CHAPTER TEN }

1) Leith's letter also reported that the Traills "both said they could have published another more melancholy story than Mrs Moodie [in *Roughing It*…] who they seemed to say had rather drawn upon her imagination for some of her facts."

2) Catharine had readily accepted Thomas's "foreign eccentricities of manner & some faults of nervous irritability of constitution" and learned to live compatibly with his depressions, and she did her best to honour the high-minded harmony that she had found in him as her husband.

3) For Richard Bentley's benefit Susanna reported in an 1855 letter that Kate Fox "… is certainly a witch, for you cannot help looking into the dreamy depths of those sweet violet eyes till you feel magnitized [sic] by them."

4) To Richard Bentley, Susanna confessed in 1856, "I have grown weary of writing idle tales, and the public seems weary of them too and I begin to feel a mortifying certainty that my style does not suit the generality of readers. It belongs like me to *the past.*"

{ CHAPTER ELEVEN }

1) When Rob Moodie's wife, Nellie, who was subject to depressions, was confined to the Toronto Asylum for a time in 1872–74, Susanna did what she could to help him with his children and the family's domestic needs. Later in the decade she stayed mostly with Rob's family in Toronto after he accepted a position in John Vickers' firm. It was only when illness overtook her in 1883 that she found her final refuge with the Vickerses.

2) James, Catharine's eldest son, died of tuberculosis in 1867. Younger sons Willie and Walter found careers with the Hudson's Bay Company.

3) In later years Agnes and Susanna resumed a rather stiff correspondence, but in her will Agnes did not leave Susanna a single memento of Reydon Hall, "which was rather mean I must say," wrote Catharine. When a box full of Agnes's clothes and jewellery arrived in Canada, Susanna received only a bracelet and a brooch.

4) Polly Cow Island was named for an Indian chief's daughter, who, according to legend, had died of a broken heart. Catharine bequeathed the island to the Peterborough Historical Society and it is now part of the Otonabee Conservation Authority.

Genealogies

Thomas Strickland
(1758–1818)

m.

(1) Susanna Butt
(d. c. 1790: no issue)

(2) Elizabeth Homer (1772–1864)

Elizabeth (Eliza) (1794–1875)	Agnes (1796–1874)	Sarah (Thay) (1798–1890) *m.* (1) Robert Childs (d. 1837) (2) Richard Gwillym (d. 1868)

Thomas Traill
(1793–1859)

m.

(1) Anne Fotheringhame (d. 1828)

(2) Catharine Parr Strickland (1802–99)

(1) > Walter (1815–1845)	John Heddle (1819–1847) *m.* Eliza Dunbar Heddle (d. 1844)	(2) > James George (1833–1867) *m.* Amelia Keye Muchall	Katherine Agnes Strickland (Kate) (1836–1922)	Thomas Henry Strickland (Hal) (1837–1870) *m.* Lilias Grant Maclean

John Wedderburn Dunbar Moodie
(1797–1869)

m.

Susanna Strickland
(1803–1885)

Catherine Mary Josephine (1832–1904) *m.* John Joseph Vickers (b. 1818)	Agnes Dunbar (1833–1913) *m.* (1) Charles Thomas Fitzgibbon (d. 1865) (2) Brown Chamberlin (1827–1897)	John Alexander Dunbar (1834–1927) *m.* Eliza Roberta Russell (1834–1882)

Jane Margaret
(1800–1888)

Catharine Parr
(1803– 1885)
m.

Thomas Traill
(1793–1859)

Susanna
(1803–1885)
m.

J.W.D. Moodie
(1797–1869)

Samuel
(1805–1867)
m.

(1) Emma Black
(d. 1826)
(2) Mary Reid
(1808–1850)
(3) Katherine
Rackham
(d. 1890)

Thomas
(1807–1874)
m.

(1) Anne
Thompson
(d. 1863)
(2) Margaretta

Anne Traill
Fotheringhame
(Annie)
(1838–1931)

m.

James Parr
Clinton
Atwood
(1836–1912)

Mary Ellen
Bridges
(1840-1841)

Mary Elizabeth
Jane
(1841–1892)

m.

Thomas
W. Muchall
(d. 1898)

Eleanor
Stewart (1843
d. infant)

William
Edward
(1844–1917)

m.

Harriette
McKay
(1847–1920)

Walter John
Strickland
(1848–1932)

m.

Mary E. Purdy

Donald
(1836– 1893)

m.

Julia Ann Russell

John Strickland
(1838–1844)

George Arthur
(19 July 1840 –
8 Aug. 1840)

Robert Baldwin
(1843–1889)

m.

Sarah Elizabeth
Russell (Nellie)
(1847–1930)

Picture Credits

Every effort has been made to clear copyright and correctly attribute all photographs. If errors have occurred we will correct them in a future edition. All images not credited here are from private collections. Unless otherwise indicated, all photography is by Ian Brewster.

AO   – Archives of Ontario
CCCM – Christ Church
           Community Museum,
           Lakefield
LAC   – Library and
           Archives Canada
NPG   – National Portrait
           Gallery, London
PCMA – Peterborough Centennial
           Museum and Archives
TPL   – Toronto Public Library
TUA   – Trent University Archives

Front jacket: Page from 1891 plant scrapbook by Catharine Parr Traill, Traill family fonds, PCMA, Acc. No. 1999-039

Back jacket: *Bush Farm near Chatham*, (c.1838) by Philip J. Bainbrigge, LAC, Acc. No. 1983-47-21 / C-011811

1: (Top) Reydon Hall illus. from *Agnes Strickland* by Una Pope-Hennessy (Bottom) Log cabin illus. from *Roughing It in the Bush* by Susanna Moodie

2-3: *Lake Katchewanook* (1867) by J.H. Caddy, courtesy of Mark and Heather Roper

5: First page of 1891 plant scrapbook by Catharine Parr Traill, Traill family fonds, PCMA, Acc. No. 1999-039

6: *Making a Road Between Kingston and York* by James Pattison Cockburn, LAC, Acc. No. 1989-255-2/ C-012630

12: Portraits of three Strickland sisters by Thomas Cheesman from *Agnes Strickland* by Una Pope-Hennessy

14: (Top) *A N.W. View of Southwold*, (1826) by H.Davy; (Bottom) *A View of Gun Hill, Southwold* (1829) by H. Davy, both courtesy of Southwold Museum and Historical Society

20: (Bottom) See page 1

21: (Left, top) *Catherine Parr* (c.1545) by unknown artist, oil on panel / NPG 4618; (bottom) *John Middleton and his Family in the Drawing Room* (c.1796) by English School 18th century, oil on canvas, © Museum of London, UK / The Bridgeman Art Library

22: (Top) *Thomas Wolsey* (c. 1520) by unknown artist, oil on panel / NPG 32

23: (Top) *The Burning of the Royal James at the Battle of Solebay, 18 May 1672*, tapestry woven by Thomas Poynz © National Maritime Museum, London / D 1987

26: (Top) Courtesy of Bungay Museum; (bottom) Phrenology chart, Image Select / Art Resource, NY/ART 123774

28: *Thomas Cheesman* (circa 1777), attributed to Francesco Bartolozzi, oil on canvas / NPG 780

29: (All images) TPL

30: (Both images) National Art Library, Victoria & Albert Museum, London

32: (Top left) *Jane Porter* (c.1811) by Samuel Freeman, stipple engraving / NPG, D9126; (Top right) *Letitia Elizabeth Landon (Mrs Maclean)*, (published 1852), by Henry Robinson, after Henry William Pickersgill, stipple engraving, NPG, D5413; (Bottom left) *John Martin* (c.1839) by Henry Warren, oil on panel, NPG 958; (Bottom right) *Sir Walter Scott, 1st Bt* (c.1824) by Sir Edwin Henry Landseer, oil on panel, NPG 391

33: *Thomas Pringle* by William Findler, stipple and line engraving, published 1837, NPG D5559

35: (Top) The British Library; (bottom) The Trustees of The British Museum, SI156589

41: (Right) First page of *Enthusiasm* poem, TPL

42: (Top right) *Signing the Marriage Register*, (1896) by James Charles (1851-1906) © Bradford Art Galleries and Museums, West Yorkshire, UK/ The Bridgeman Art Library

45: TUA

48: *Southwold, Suffolk* (1822) by William Daniell, courtesy of Southwold Museum and Historical Society

50: (Top) Doug Houghton Photography

51: (All images) Doug Houghton Photography

52: Kendrick, Charles, *Canadian Illustrated News*, 14 September, 1872 / LAC

53: *Canadian Illustrated News*, 02 July, 1870 / LAC

54: *View of Quebec from the St. Lawrence River* (c.1870) by Edmund Willoughby Sewell / LAC, Acc. No. 1991-120-4/ C-011045

56: *Notre Dame Street, Montreal* (1843) by John Murray / M970.67.23 © McCord Museum

58: *At Foot of Jacques Cartier Square, Montreal* (1840) by William Workman/MP-0000.817.2 © McCord Museum

60: (Right, top) The Rare Books & Special Collections Division, McGill University, *Illustrated London News*, 1847; (right, middle) *Illustrated London News*, May 10, 1851 / C-006556 / LAC; (left, bottom) Parks Canada / H. Boucher

61: (Top) Parks Canada/J. Beardsell; (bottom) Parks Canada/H. Boucher

63: *Cobourg, Lake Ontario* (1840) by Philip John Bainbrigge, (1817-1881), LAC, Acc. No. 1983-47-78 / C-011865

64: (Top) *View near the head of the St. Lawrence River* (1830) by Thomas Burrowes, AO, Ref. Code: C 1-0-0-0-92, Thomas Burrowes fonds; (Bottom) *View of the St. Lawrence River in the Lake of a Thousand Islands* (1830) by Thomas Burrowes, AO, Ref. Code: C1-0-0-0-90 Thomas Burrowes fonds.

67: (Top) TUA; (bottom) *Canadian Illustrated News*, 13 October, 1877, LAC / C-066090

68: *Log House and Clearing near Orillia* (c.1844) by Titus Hibbert Ware (1810-1890), LAC, Acc. No. R9266-403 Peter Winkworth Collection of Canadiana / C-151563

69: Map by Jack McMaster

71: (Top) *Otonabee River at Peterboro [sic]* (1837) by Anne Langton, AO, Ref. Code: F 1077-8-1-4-15, John Langton fonds; (bottom) *On the Otonobee [River] near Peterboro [sic]* (c. 1852) by Anne Langton, watercolour, AO, Ref. Code: F 1077-8-1-2-27, John Langton fonds.

72: (Top) *Sleighing in the Country* (1842) by Sir Henry James Warre, brown wash over paper, LAC, Acc. No. 1965-76-49 / C-023073; (bottom) PCMA

74-75: (Top) Silhouette and map, TUA; (bottom) Archives Rare Book Collection, PCMA, Acc. No. 1995-058

77: *Bush Farm near Chatham*, (c.1838) by Philip J. Bainbrigge, LAC, Acc. No. 1983-47-21 / C-011811

79: *Home built by Sergeant-Major William McCracken of the 18th*

Royal Regiment in Dummer Township in 1832, hand-tinted photograph from the Denne family fonds (67-40-4), PCMA, Acc. No. 1978-012

81: *Lake Katchewanook* (1867) by J.H. Caddy, (detail), courtesy of Mark and Heather Roper

82: (Top) *Uncle Waish-ky's Lodge at the Sault Ste. Marie* by Anna Jameson; *ROM2006-7103-1*, Royal Ontario Museum © ROM; (middle) *Squaws of the Chippewa tribe (after a work in "Indian Portraits" entitled Squaws of Chippewa tribe painted at Treaty of Fond du Lac*, by J.O. Lewis, (1826) [1847] AO, C 281-0-0-0-59, Documentary Art Collection. (Bottom) Canoe, courtesy of PCMA.

84-85: Baldwin Room, TPL

86: Photo courtesy of Kathy Hooke

88: *Photograph of a drawing of William Lyon Mackenzie (1795-1861)* [n.d], AO S 2123

89: *Sir Francis Bond Head, Bart., KCH* [Lieutenant Governor of Upper Canada, 1836-38] [c. 1883] Archives of Ontario, 606899, Berthon, George Theodore, Government of Ontario Art Collection

90: (Top) *Rebellion Banner*, 1837 AO / F 37, AO 4565; (bottom) *The March of the Rebels upon Toronto in December, 1837* [c. 1921] AO, 621229, Jefferys, Charles William (C.W.), Government of Ontario Art Collection

92: (Left, top) *John Lovell, Montreal, QC, (1865)* I-19133.1 © McCord Museum; (right, top) *The Literary Garland and British North American Magazine* M930.51.1.431 © McCord Museum

93: *Major-General Sir George Arthur, Bart., KCB* [Lieutenant Governor of Upper Canada, 1838-41] [c. 1887], artist unknown, after

SMART, Government of Ontario art collection, AO / 693137

94: Illustration by Lynne Clifford-Ward, courtesy of Hutchison House Museum, Peterborough

95: All images courtesy of Hutchison House Museum

97: Books from CCCM

99: *Lord Durham* [ca. 1800] AO, RG 49-33-0-0-18, Ontario Legislative Library Print Collection

100: *The Hastings County Court House and Gaol, Belleville* (1870) by George Ackermann, (CAG 98.5.1), The Confederation Centre Art Gallery, Charlottetown

101: Detail from photo on p.145

102: (Top) *Belleville at the mouth of the Moira River, Bay of Quinte* [1830], AO, C 1-0-0-0-109, Thomas Burrowes fonds; (middle) *Belleville, Looking East* [1830] AO, C 1-0-0-0-110, Thomas Burrowes fonds; (bottom) *Moira River at Belleville* [1830] (AO, C 1-0-0-0-108, Thomas Burrowes fonds.

103: (Left) *Agnes Strickland* (1846) by John Hayes, oil on canvas, NPG 403; (right, top) *Queen Victoria* (1819-1901) (litho) (b/w photo) by English School (19th century) © The Illustrated London News Picture Library, London, UK/ The Bridgeman Art Library; (bottom) From *Agnes Strickland* by Una Pope-Hennessy

105: George Bridges photo courtesy of TUA.

106: (Top) *Rice Lake From the Church at Gore's Landing* by F.J Rowan, ROM2003-854-7; Royal Ontario Museum © ROM; (bottom) Illustration by Jack McMaster

107: *Cedar Swamp, Rice Lake* (1850) by Marie Harvey, courtesy of Mrs. Pauline Pengelley Northey

108: Courtesy of Glanmore National Historic Site

109: *George Benjamin, M.P.,* (1859) by William Sawyer (1820-1889), oil on canvas, 101.6 x 76.2m. Courtesy of Glanmore National Historic Site

110: (Top) *The Honourable Robert Baldwin* [ca. 1840] AO, C 281-0-0-0-144, Archives of Ontario Documentary Art Collection

115: (Top) Page from Minute Book, courtesy of Glanmore National Historic Site

116-117: Photographs by David Acomba

118: *Photograph of Susanna Moodie*, LAC / C-007043

119: PCMA, Howard Pammett fonds Acc. No. 1989-001

120: Traill family / Library and Archives Canada / C-067346

121: (see p. 119)

122: (Left and right, top) (see p. 119); (right, bottom) CCCM

123: (see p. 119)

124: (Left) TUA; (right) *Richard Bentley* (1844) by Charles Baugniet, lithograph, NPG / D11247

125: TPL

126: CCCM

127: (Top) PCMA Rare Book Collection, Acc. No. 1995-058; (bottom) TPL

128: (Right inset, top & bottom) TPL

130: Photo courtesy of TUA

131: (Left, top) Sam Strickland photo courtesy of TUA; (right, top) Lakefield illlus. by P.W.G Canning, *Canadian Illustrated News*, 04 September, 1875 / LAC; (right, middle) Homestead photo, Traill Family Collection, LAC / C-067335

132: Photograph by David Acomba

133: *The Log House on Rice Lake* by Charles Fothergill, watercolour; ROM2003_854_6, Royal Ontario Museum © ROM

135: National Library of Canada / LAC

137: (All images) Central Library of Rochester & Monroe County

138: (Top, right) Spiritualist Diary, LAC / nlc-1426; (bottom) TPL Picture Collection

140: (Top left) Photo coutesy of Kathy Hooke

142: (Left) Agnes Strickland by Alfred Brothers, albumen carte-de-visite, 1860s, NPG Ax46423

145: Photo courtesy of Gerry Boyce

147: CCCM

148: *Mrs. Susannah Moodie, Montreal, QC*, 1866, I-23581.1 © McCord Museum

149: *Mr. John Moodie, Montreal, QC*, 1866, I-23203.1 © McCord Museum

150: (Top) Traill Family Collection / LAC / PA-201403; (bottom) Traill Family Collection / LAC / NL-17457

151: (Top) LAC / C-067343; (bottom) CCCM

152: (Left) TUA; (right, top, middle & bottom) CCCM

153: (Top) PCMA; (bottom) CCCM

154: (Top) LAC / C-067338

155: CCCM

156: CCCM

157: (Top, left) Topley Studio / LAC / PA-013248; (top, right) H. Spencer / LAC / C-000606; (bottom) Pittaway & Jarvis / LAC / C-003812

160: Traill Family Collection / LAC / C-067327

161: LAC / PA-117832

162: (Top) Topley Studio / LAC / PA-026304; (bottom) PCMA, Acc. No. 1968-001

176: Photograph by David Acomba

Quotation Sources

Most of the direct quotations in the text and sidebars of this book are either from *Roughing it in the Bush, The Backwoods of Canada* or other works by Moodie and Traill. The excerpts from their letters are from the three volumes of letters I edited along with Carl Ballstadt and Elizabeth Hopkins: *Susanna Moodie: Letters of a Lifetime* (1985); *Letters of Love and Duty: The Correspondence of John and Susanna Moodie* (1993); and *I Bless You in My Heart: Selected Correspondence of Catharine Parr Traill* (1996). The poems by Susanna on pages 10 and 92 are from *Roughing it in the Bush* while 'The Early Lost' on page 112 is from *Life in the Clearings*. Agnes Strickland's poem on page 17 is from her 1827 collection, *The Seven Ages of Woman and other Poems*. I have also excerpted from Una Pope-Hennessey's *Agnes Strickland: Biographer of the Queens of England* (1940) and from Catharine Parr Traill's "A Slight Sketch of the Early Life of Mrs. Moodie" and "Rice Lake Plains — The Wolf Tower" both included in *Forest and Other Gleanings*. Annie Traill's recollections of Wolf Tower are part of the Traill Family Collection at Library and Archives Canada which also houses the Patrick Hamilton Ewing Collection of Moodie material and the Susanna Moodie Collection.

— *Michael Peterman*

Bibliography

Ballstadt, Carl, Hopkins, Elizabeth and Peterman, Michael, editors. *Susanna Moodie: Letters of a Lifetime*. Toronto: University of Toronto Press, 1985.

———— *Letters of Love and Duty: The Correspondence of John and Susanna Moodie*. Toronto: University of Toronto Press, 1993.

———— *I Bless You in My Heart: Selected Correspondence of Catharine Parr Traill*. Toronto: University of Toronto Press, 1996.

Fowler, Marian. *The Embroidered Tent: Five Gentlewomen in Early Canada*. Toronto: House of Anansi Press Limited, 1982.

Gray, Charlotte. *Sisters in the Wilderness: The Lives of Susanna Moodie and Catharine Parr Traill*. Toronto: Penguin Books Canada Limited, 1999.

Martin, Norma, Milne, Catherine and McGillis, Donna. *Gore's Landing and the Rice Lake Plains*. Gore's Landing: Heritage Gore's Landing, 1986.

Morris, Audrey. *Gentle Pioneers*. Toronto and London: Hodder and Stoughton, 1966.

Peterman, Michael. *Susanna Moodie: A Life*. Toronto: ECW Press, 1999.

————, and Carl Ballstadt, editors. *Forest and Other Gleanings: The Fugitive Writings of Catharine Parr Traill*. Ottawa: University of Ottawa Press, 1994.

Pope-Hennessey, Una. *Agnes Strickland: Biographer of the Queens of England*. London: Chatto & Windus, 1940.

Strickland, Jane Margaret. *Life of Agnes Strickland*. London: William Blackwood and Sons, 1887.

Thurston, John, editor. *Voyages: Short Narratives of Susanna Moodie*. Ottawa: University of Ottawa Press, 1991.

————, *The Work of Words: The Writings of Susanna Strickland Moodie*. Montreal: McGill-Queens University Press, 1996.

Tames, Richard. *Bloomsbury Past*. London: Historical Publications Limited, 1993.

———— *Clerkenwell and Finsbury Past*. London: Historical Publications Limited, 1999.

Index

To Cara, Rob and Jessie
— M.P.

Acknowledgements

WE ARE INDEBTED TO MANY PEOPLE ON BOTH SIDES OF THE ATLANTIC FOR their help with this book. First off, I'd like to thank my wife, Cara, my assistant, Wendy Scammell, and my longstanding editorial colleagues, Elizabeth Hopkins and Carl Ballstadt. In London, we'd like to thank Sian Phillips for books and advice; Adrian Smith of Cameron Mackintosh Ltd. for his help with photography at No.1 Bedford Square. Thanks also to the occupants of Leverton House and to Hampstead historian Christopher Wade. In Southwold, we're indebted to Raymond LeGrys for allowing us to photograph at Reydon Hall, to Paul Scriven of the Southwold Museum and Historical Society, and to the churchwardens of St. Margaret's, Reydon, St. Edmund's, Southwold and the Wrentham Chapel. Thanks also to Christopher Reeve of the Bungay Museum. In the Orkneys, thanks to Doug Houghton for his photographs, and to Elsie Seatter of Melsetter.

In Peterborough, Ontario, we're grateful to Bernadine Dodge and Jodi Aoki at the Trent University Archives, to the staff of the Peterborough Centennial Museum and Archives (www.pcma.ca), to Gale Fewings of the Hutchison House Museum, and also former curator, Lynne Clifford-Ward, to local historian Kathy Hooke, and to Mark and Heather Roper. In Lakefield, special thanks to Jean Murray Cole of the Christ Church Community Museum for advice and photography, to Moira and Ted Collins for the tour of Westove, and to the staff of Lang Pioneer Village. On the Rice Lake Plains we're indebted to Donna McGillis for her consultation and a tour of the south shore, and to Doreen and David Lander for the hike around the Wolf Tower site. We're also very grateful to David Acomba and Sharon Keogh for showing us Mount Ararat and for David's splendid photography with matching quotes sourced by Sharon. Pauline Pengelley Northey and her daughter Dori Northey kindly allowed us to photograph the family's 1850 watercolour of Rice Lake. In Belleville, Gerry Boyce was our guide to the town and the Moodie gravesite. Special thanks to Jackie and Leo Simpson for permitting us to photograph at the Moodie cottage. At Glanmore National Historic Site, Rona Rustige and Melissa Wakeling provided access to artifacts and allowed us to photograph them. Thanks also to Lisa Ellenwood of the CBC, and to Fiona O'Connor of the Toronto Public Library. Particular thanks are due to Charlotte Gray for her excellent introduction, to Gord Sibley for his book design, and to Ian Brewster for his photography in two worlds. At Doubleday Canada, we would like to thank Brad Martin and Maya Mavjee for acquiring the book, Lara Hinchberger for text editing, and Susan Burns for shepherding the book so smoothly and carefully.

"All through the winter you may see the bright ruby fruit upon the bushes, among the snow-clad branches, sometimes encased in crystal ice and magnified by the magic touch of hoar-frost."

— Catharine Parr Traill,
Studies of Plant Life in Canada

Project Editor: Hugh Brewster

Book Design: Gordon Sibley

Photography: Ian Brewster
David Acomba
Doug Houghton

Maps & Diagrams: Jack McMaster

Editorial Assistance: Laurie Coulter
Lloyd Davis
Kim Folliott

Production: Bill Rose

Printing and Binding: Oceanic Graphic
Printing Ltd.

SISTERS *in* TWO WORLDS
was produced by
Whitfield Editions Ltd.